Praise for
To Be Told
by Dan B. Allender

"This is a book worth reading. Because this is a journey worth taking. To know who you are. To make sense of your life. To discover the role God is giving you in his story. That is a life worth living. Thank you, Dan, for a wonderful book!"

— JOHN ELDREDGE, best-selling author of *Wild at Heart* and *Epic: The Story God Is Telling and the Role That Is Yours to Play*

"Dan Allender's books brim and sizzle with stories—many poignant, many hilarious, and many both. This book takes us to the deepest stories of all—our own stories, the ones that haunt when they are kept secret and liberate when they are told and known. *To Be Told* is a treasure to be read slowly and with your closest friends."

— BRIAN MCLAREN, pastor and author of *A Generous Orthodoxy* and *A New Kind of Christian*

"The concepts in this book have helped define my life in magnificent ways. By further exploring my own story, I discovered God's story. And it is a beautiful picture of clarity, purpose, knowledge, and celebration. Thank you, God, for giving us Dan Allender."

— KATHY TROCCOLI, singer, speaker, and author

"When Dan Allender tells stories, prepare for three things: laughter, tears, and piercing insight. Allender is a great storyteller because he knows that stories are for redeeming, not just for passing the time. This book, about story and full of stories, will help you find your own place in the greatest story ever told."

— DANIEL TAYLOR, author of *Tell Me a Story: The Life-Shaping Power of Our Stories*

"Dan Allender confronts us with the truth that we are storied people, that each of us is a story, and that we are in fact writing our own stories. With humor and grace, Dan invites us not only to write our stories metaphorically but literally to begin to write our stories. He promises that in so doing we might just possibly find God, with whom we are coauthoring our stories, and we might actually connect in vital and healing ways with ourselves and with each other."
　　—STANLEY J. GRENZ, author of *Rediscovering the Triune God*
　　and *A Primer on Postmodernism*

"In *To Be Told,* Dan Allender creates an intimate, safe place where we feel free to join in the discussion and dive, with a sort of careless courage, headfirst into our own stories. I wept as I rediscovered the sacred and divine in my own story, and began to find the connections between my own story threads, an understanding of my long-aching need to be heard, and the glimmers of a holy redemption."
　　—RENEE ALTSON, author of *Stumbling Toward Faith*

"Dan Allender calls us to recognize that our lives, which often seem random, have a brilliant, divine coherence. Under his expert tutelage we discover how to discern God's hand on our lives and how to tell the story to ourselves and others."
　　—TREMPER LONGMAN III, author of *How to Read the Psalms*
　　and coauthor of *The Cry of the Soul* and *Bold Love*

to be told workbook

KNOW YOUR STORY • SHAPE YOUR FUTURE

Dan B. Allender, PhD
and Lisa K. Fann, MA

WATERBROOK
PRESS

TO BE TOLD WORKBOOK
PUBLISHED BY WATERBROOK PRESS
2375 Telstar Drive, Suite 160
Colorado Springs, Colorado 80920
A division of Random House, Inc.

Details in some anecdotes and stories have been changed to protect the identities of the persons involved.

ISBN 1-57856-949-4

Printed in the United States of America
2005—First Edition

10 9 8 7 6 5 4 3 2 1

Contents

> *"Since the beginning of time all humanity has been wrapped in a mothers security blanket."*

Nellie Thomas

introduction

Your picking up this workbook suggests you've already started a journey into stories. Perhaps you're looking for meaning in your suffering, or maybe you're curious about what your life adds up to. Perhaps something inside you quietly insists that there has to be more to life.

yes - I am seeking the reason that I have been put here on earth - where can I make a difference?

You've probably looked skeptically at the path back through stories and wondered whether it's even worth traveling. Many reluctant pilgrims will argue, *I already walked through that. The past is the past; there's no reason to rehash it. What benefit could possibly come from walking back into those stories?*

They have a point. Too often we tell our stories poorly. We tell our stories without curiosity and create only boredom. We tell them without honesty and add another layer of shellac to an already idealized past. We tell them without gentleness and weave tales of vengeance against ourselves and others. By telling our stories poorly, we dishonor them and mire ourselves in anger and contempt. No wonder the reluctant pilgrims argue so vehemently against looking at the past. Often they have struggled and toiled to leave the past behind. What could possibly induce someone to sully the present by dredging up old stories?

The problem is that, as someone once said, if we don't tell our stories, our stories will tell us. Whether we revisit the past or not, who we are today is profoundly shaped by the events of our lives and our responses to those events. Our stories impact us either unconsciously or consciously. It's up to us to decide whether we'll be passive recipients or active agents in the shaping of our lives.

Choosing to engage our stories honestly requires a great deal of courage. How much easier it is to let life happen to us. In the insanity of our busy days, we don't make time to reflect on our lives. We stumble or jog as well as possible along the path, pressed on by the urgencies of life: advancing in our jobs, taxiing the kids around, serving in our churches. If we were to step off the trail and sit for a moment under a tree, the cost would likely be enormous—either in time, money, or disappointed expectations of others. What would cause us to be crazy enough to do that? Simply, that quiet voice that calls us to more.

Socrates once said that the unexamined life is not worth living.[1] One of the privileges of being human is that we have an enormous capacity to reflect and learn and change. When we settle for simply getting by, we mar the glory that was created in us and we thwart the potential for growth and maturity. Choosing a richer life requires revisiting the past, which may reopen painful wounds of failure and betrayal. The only reason worth reentering that pain is the hope that somehow it can be transformed, that through it we will learn to love better and will know more joy. We trudge through the valley of the shadow of death clinging to the hope of what lies on the other side. We could take the shortcut of putting the past behind us and leaving it there. But instead we choose the difficult path back through stories because of our sacred hope that this path will lead to something beautiful and good: *God has a history of redeeming. Perhaps he will redeem my stories as well.*

The path won't be easy. In this hike through the wilderness of our lives and hearts, we will be truly alive only if we feel the rain and sleet on our faces, the jagged rocks beneath our feet, and the relentless heat of the sun. Only then will we be able to enjoy fully the brilliant colors of the flowers, the stirring of our hair in the breeze, and the crispness of a fall evening. The bitterness makes the sweet that much sweeter. When we avoid suffering, we rob ourselves of joy.

So, as we journey through stories, we hope for a deeper taste of joy and a glimpse of redemption. We are detectives searching for the fingerprints of God in our lives. We look for traces of his authorship in the rubble of a fallen world. In David Wilcox's song "Show the Way," he tells of a play where it looks as if the hero arrived too late: "In this scene set in shadows… / There is evil cast around us / But it's love that wrote the play."[2] We embark on this journey because we believe—or at least we hope—that love wrote our lives despite what it might seem at times. We choose to believe—or at least hope— that our lives consist of more than simply a series of events. Underneath and through each scene lies the hint of a larger story that God is telling through our lives. Some meanings may remain hidden to us until we get to heaven. Other meanings slowly reveal the way God has uniquely gifted us to do his work.

God, our great Author, created us in his image. One aspect of this is our inventiveness. We cannot create in the same way God did, for God created out of nothing. But God has given us the raw materials and invited us to make something both unique and beautiful. On the sixth day, God finished creating us, but he did not finish writing our lives. We are called to participate with him in this writing. Our journey involves a search for the places where God hands us the pen and invites us to write.

But why write? the reluctant pilgrim will ask. *Can I not simply tell my stories to someone?* Telling and writing stories are two very different acts. Both are important. As you embark on any journey, it is wise to choose trustworthy companions who will listen to your stories with both tenderness and strength, who will encourage you when the path becomes difficult. Telling our stories to one another leads to richer, deeper relationships. But writing our stories can make them more real. There is something safe in the transitory nature of speech. Sound dissipates; pen strokes do not. Writing requires a different level of commitment and offers rich rewards.

By writing your stories, you begin to see them in a different way. Details that you almost forgot suddenly stand out, and you begin to make connections that eluded you when you spoke the tale. Metaphors take on a life of their own, and themes become more pronounced. Stories reveal themselves to be something other than what you thought. You can talk and walk at the same time, but writing forces you to step off the path and sit under a tree so you can ponder.

May we never dredge up the past to harm others or simply to avoid the present by reliving the past. The purpose in going back is to look more closely, to notice more carefully the scenery and the direction of the path. The first time you walked the path, you were moving too quickly to take in everything. You were trying to fix dinner or study math or mow the lawn while life was happening. Memory makes it possible for us to revisit our days and learn what we missed the first time around.

This is your invitation to walk back through the stories of your life. The path won't be easy. You will revisit the perilous river crossings, the brutal deserts, and the steep mountain switchbacks as well as the peaceful meadows and refreshing forest streams. Traveling the path back through stories will lead to moments of both joy and sorrow.

We are honored to be your traveling companions. May you tell your stories with curiosity, honesty, and gentleness.

chapter one

the view from thirty thousand feet

> Did you ever think, child…how much piecin' a quilt's like livin' a
> life?… You see, you start out with jest so much caliker; you don't go to
> the store and pick it out and buy it, but the neighbors will give you a
> piece here and a piece there, and you'll have a piece left every time you
> cut out a dress, and you take jest what happens to come. And that's like
> predestination. But when it comes to the cuttin' out, why, you're free to
> choose your own pattern. You can give the same kind o' pieces to two
> persons, and one'll make a "nine-patch" and one'll make a "wild-goose
> chase," and there'll be two quilts made out o' the same kind o' pieces,
> and jest as different as they can be. And that is jest the way with livin'.
> The Lord sends us the pieces, but we can cut 'em out and put 'em
> together pretty much to suit ourselves, and there's a heap more in the
> cuttin' out and the sewin' than there is in the caliker.
> —ELIZA CALVERT HALL, *Aunt Jane of Kentucky*

The prospect of writing stories from your life can feel as if you're making a quilt from
a jumbled pile of calico scraps. You pick up a couple of pieces and look at them skeptically. *Where do I start? Will this really be worth the time it takes? Why bother with stitch-
ing a quilt when I can just buy a blanket and be done with it?*

The beauty of creating a quilt (or any other piece of art) in our prefabricated world is that it reveals so much *about* the artist and *to* the artist. As Aunt Jane suggests, quilts, like stories, show the personality of the one who pieces them together. A work of art can also reveal something that the artist didn't realize he or she already knew. Through the process of creating, we come to understand ourselves more fully. Aunt Jane's quilt making describes a strange truth: we construct our lives and have our lives given to us. In writing our stories, we search for patterns, themes, and ultimately redemption. We search for truth.

> When a day passes, it is no longer there. What remains of it? Nothing more than a story. If stories weren't told or books weren't written, man would live like the beasts, only for the day.... Today we live, but by tomorrow today will be a story. The whole world, all human life, is one long story.
>
> —Isaac Bashevis Singer, *Naftali the Storyteller and His Horse, Sus, and Other Stories*

Someone once said that God created humans because he loves stories. And the Old Testament tells us about God through the narratives about his people. Jesus told stories and is himself the story of God's outrageous love for us. Stories make up more than 70 percent of the Bible, and it is in the stories of our lives that we can spot God's handiwork. The blank spaces in this workbook are waiting for your stories, the places where you've seen God's presence and the places where you've experienced his absence. We'll start slowly, with snippets and small pieces. Then we'll look at a few scenes more closely and search for commonalities and themes. From these we'll look for an overarching direction to your life, ways that God is transforming you through your pain and equipping you uniquely to bring comfort and hope to others.

In Mary Oliver's poem "The Summer Day," she writes:

Doesn't everything die at last, and too soon?
Tell me, what is it you plan to do
with your one wild and precious life?[1]

This workbook is designed to help you answer that question by looking closely at your life. If this all feels too quick, remember that you can go as slowly as you desire.

More than a century ago a wise woman likened life to making a quilt—and you don't make a quilt in a day.

We are quilt makers, artists, explorers. As you work through this book, use whatever metaphor makes sense to you. The point is to see your life differently. You can think of this workbook as a hiking guide that points out trails, places to find potable water, campsites, dangerous drop-offs, and beautiful vistas. Some of the directions may not be helpful; some of the trails may be of little interest to you. Skip those sections. Look instead for the paths you might have missed that will make your journey richer. The questions are designed to help you ponder in greater depth the ideas presented in the book *To Be Told* by Dan B. Allender. Start by reading chapter 1, "The Tale to Be Told," as you begin this workbook.

Writing offers a unique opportunity to make connections and gain greater clarity. If this is a trail guide, it is one that you write. As you answer the questions and write your stories, don't worry about unimportant details like grammar and spelling. The point is to look honestly at your heart, not to win a writing competition. If the task begins to overwhelm you, allot yourself a certain amount of time (say, forty-five minutes) to write. When the timer rings, you can put down your pen or turn off the computer. If the number of questions feels daunting, write short phrases for your answers or skip some of the questions. We've used asterisks to mark the questions that we feel are most important to answer. If you want to do just the minimum, begin with those. So that you will feel free to write honestly about what you are feeling, find a safe place to keep this book so others won't read it. And allow yourself the freedom to put the book away for a while if you need to do so. The journey lasts a lifetime, and God is patient with us.

WHERE ARE YOU RIGHT NOW?

An important part of any journey or work of art is to mark where you begin so later you can look back at how far you've come. Start this process by answering the following questions.

1. When you were growing up, when did your family tell stories? Who told them? Example: *At family gatherings my aunts and uncles told stories about the chaos of growing up in a family with nine kids.*

2. When do you tell stories now? How important are stories in your family?

3. What kinds of stories are told in your family? What stories are off limits?

4. How do you feel when you think about writing some of the stories of your life? Are you excited? anxious? overwhelmed? eager? skeptical?

5. What people in your life would be displeased if they knew you were writing stories? List the comments and arguments that each person would likely make. Include anyone who comes to mind even if that person is dead. Example: *Maternal grandmother: "You're just like your Aunt Allison, trying to stir up trouble by rehashing things. There is no reason to go airing out our dirty laundry."*

6. List all the things that might hinder you from writing truthfully or writing at all. Examples: *I don't want to revisit some very painful events. Writing takes so long and feels unproductive.*

Your Well of Stories

This workbook invites you to write down stories (scenes, really) from your life. You can use your own journal or a spiral notebook or a computer to record your stories as you work through this book. We'll start by listing all the stories you can remember. Whether these stories come in a flood or a trickle, the well will hold them. You will dip into this well of stories later as you begin to write. (Please note that we use the words *story* and *scene* interchangeably. The stories you will write are like scenes in a play. We also refer to *your story*, which is the collection of all the stories/scenes of your life, like a novel.)

> Time's covetousness is forever. Time devours and devours—and gives back nothing. How terrible to face death without ever having claimed freedom, even in all its danger!
>
> —Frederick Nietzsche, in Irvin Yalom, *When Nietzsche Wept*

To begin the list, think about the stories that you tell and the stories that others tell about you. It may help to think in terms of general categories. For each category, jot down words or phrases that help you recall scenes from your life. For example, using the category of *age,* walk through your life chronologically, remembering what life was like when you were four, seven, thirteen, nineteen, twenty-five, forty, and so on.

What is to give light must endure burning.

—VIKTOR FRANKL,
Man's Search for Meaning

7. *Age.* What is your earliest memory? What was it like to go to first grade? What was a typical day in high school like? What was your first job?

8. *Location.* What was it like to live in your neighborhood? How was your room decorated? Whom did you talk to on the school bus? Where did you live after you moved out of your childhood home?

9. *Activity.* What games did you play as a child? What are your favorite activities now? How did your parents play with you? What was it like to be a Boy Scout, Girl Scout, athlete, class president, nerd, band or choir member?

10. *People.* Who were your friends in high school? What nicknames did you have as you were growing up? Who took care of you when you were sick? Who has been a bad influence on you? Which relative have you been told you are "just like"? Why? Who has most impacted your life? Why? How did you meet your spouse?

11. *Event.* What did you do at your birthday parties? What were family vacations like? How did your family celebrate Christmas? How did your parents respond when you misbehaved? What was it like to see your child go off to kindergarten or college? How has illness or injury impacted your life? How did you respond to the events of September 11, 2001?

12. *Weather.* What did you do when it rained? What happened when school was canceled because of snow? What was your favorite season when you were growing up?

13. *Object.* How did you learn to ride a bike? What was your favorite toy? book? What kind of car did your family have? How did you dress when you were a teenager? What was the first music album, tape, or CD that you bought?

14. *Time of day or year.* In your family, what was the atmosphere around the dinner table? What did you do when you arrived home from school? What did you do during the summer? What bedtime rituals did you have as a child?

15. *Emotion.* What was the best day of your life? What makes you angry? When were you betrayed? When have you felt powerless? What was your most embarrassing moment? your most glorious moment?

16. *Beliefs.* What did your parents believe about God? When in your life did you feel most spiritually bereft? What has most impacted your religious beliefs?

You can also spark your memory by thinking through the five senses. What sights, sounds, tastes, smells, and sensations of touch have left a lasting impression on you? What are the stories behind them?

17. *Sight.* Think about a drive in the country or the mountains…a friend's face…a prized possession that you lost…finding a snake in your yard…your dog playing fetch. Describe the visual images that come to mind.

18. *Sound.* Imagine hearing the wind in the trees, laughter, your favorite CD, your mother's voice, chalk on a chalkboard, a gunshot, frogs in a pond, traffic, hospital machinery, a phone ringing, whispers, a siren, a hymn. What events or feelings do you associate with these sounds?

19. *Taste.* Macaroni and cheese, ice cream, cough syrup, coffee, mangoes, a popsicle, an expensive meal in a restaurant—where do certain flavors take you?

20. *Smell.* What do you think of when you imagine smells like chocolate-chip cookies baking in the oven, pine trees, the ocean, the trash, your aunt's perfume, Thanksgiving dinner, roses, or car exhaust?

21. *Touch.* What do you associate with the feel of things like your cat, mud pies, your grandfather's lap, playing tag, your child's face, vinyl car seats, satin, a mug of hot tea, a stubbed toe?

22. Using the words and phrases that you jotted down under the preceding categories, create your well of stories on the pages of your journal. Start by making a list of ten to fifteen scenes from your life, writing a few short phrases or sentences that will help you remember the scene in greater detail.

*23. You may find it easier to think of stories more organically. Think about the topic of each of the stories that you listed in your journal. On a blank page, write down these topics (for example: loneliness, joy, abandonment, rebelliousness) in various places. Then, as you remember related stories, write them near each of the story topics like spokes extending from the hub of a wheel or shoots of crabgrass. If those stories remind you of other stories, add a new spoke or shoot. By doing this you should end up with dozens of stories to add to your well of stories.

> Religion is not to go to God by forsaking the world but by finding him in it.
> —Monk Soen Shaku

24. Look back over the list of scenes you wrote in your journal. What do the scenes have in common? For example, did you focus on fond memories of childhood or only on the tragic events of your life? What other types of gaps, such as periods of time for which you don't have any stories, do you notice? What types of stories did you avoid altogether? List the categories you missed.

25. In response to question 24, fill in some of the missing scenes. Include all sorts of stories: delightful, painful, confusing, tender, brutal, secret, triumphant.

Become a collector of stories. As you work through this book and additional stories come to mind, add them to your list. If you drop the bucket into your story well and it clanks on the bottom, you may need to do some digging. Try wandering through an antique shop or thrift store. Often you will see items from the years of your childhood that spark memories. Talk to people who knew you when you were in elementary school. Ask your friends about their childhoods and use their memories to trigger your own. Watch an old television program or read a book that you loved when you were a child. Eat cookies and milk. Revisit places you used to live or where you went to school.

What Do You Want to Accomplish?

We live in a fallen world. Even if you have known only kind, generous people, you still have been marred by cultural, national, and global evil. Writing your stories honestly will require an enormous amount of courage and perseverance. So it will be helpful to remind yourself of what you hope to accomplish through this process. The previous questions were designed to help you think about where you are right now. But what are your dreams? Where do you want to go with your stories?

To determine what you want to accomplish, ask yourself:

26. What would you like to see changed…

    about yourself?

    about your relationships with others?

    about your relationship with God?

27. What are the biggest obstacles you face? When would you be most tempted to give up?

28. Reread the lines from Mary Oliver's poem earlier in this chapter. What do you hope for?

29. Knowing that this storytelling process is never easy, what will you do to protect your writing time and your stories?

In each chapter of this workbook, you will be invited to write a story or two on a particular topic. Whether you write these stories on a computer or a pad of paper, leave space between the lines for making changes and additions. Aim for your stories to be three hundred to one thousand words long.

*30. Take five minutes to write a story from your childhood about a family vacation or your favorite pet. Don't read the next question until you've finished.

*31. Now think through what the vacation revealed about family dynamics or what your pet meant to you. Spend ten minutes rewriting your story to reflect that insight. Then compare the two versions.

Using This Workbook in a Story Group

Although you can work through this book alone, consider meeting with others to hear their feedback and perspectives on your stories. Being part of a story group also gives you a chance to enter into other people's stories. Storytelling is meant to be a communal activity. By looking at our stories through the eyes of others, we learn more about ourselves. If you do choose to meet with a group, you may want to limit the size to no more than eight people. If you have more than that, the storytelling will take too long. Plan on meeting for at least two hours each time.

> The real voyage of discovery consists not in seeking new landscapes, but in having new eyes.
>
> —Marcel Proust,
> *Remembrance of Things Past*

At each meeting, discuss a couple of questions from the workbook and then allow time for each person to read a scene from her or his life. Because of the dynamics of how stories can play off one another, it will be most helpful if everyone reads a story on the topic suggested at the end of each chapter. However, sometimes the topic won't capture your interest, while another story pesters you to write it. If so, feel free to read the story that elicits the most passion from you, keeping the length to one thousand words or fewer.

Telling your life stories to a group can be frightening and exposing. When you tell your stories, you are inviting others to walk into your life just as others are inviting you into theirs. Be sensitive and compassionate as you listen to the stories of others.

Some ground rules to consider:

- *Listen well.* Don't interrupt the storyteller. Instead, allow the words to wash over you. At the end of the story, you can offer feedback about what stood out to you. What did the story reveal to you about the teller? about the other characters? about God?
- *Maintain confidentiality.* If your story group is not a safe place for people to tell about their lives, it will disintegrate. Nothing that is said in the group should be repeated outside the group.
- *Encourage depth and honor what is offered.* The group's potential is only as deep as the stories that are told. A group characterized by light, happy stories offers you a pleasant way to spend an evening, but it will provide little opportunity to grow. Take risks by telling more difficult stories. At the same time, do not tell the stories that are most precious or most painful to you until the group has built significant trust.

FOR DISCUSSION IN YOUR STORY GROUP—MEETING 1

Read aloud the quote from Aunt Jane at the beginning of this chapter.

1. What kind of calico have you been given for your life? What are the colors and patterns? Are the scraps new? frayed? faded? colorful? attractive?
2. What does your life-quilt look like? Have you caught glimpses of what it might look like when it's finished? What patterns do you see emerging?

3. When, if ever, have you been aware of your role in cutting and sewing the pieces for your life-quilt? If you weren't previously aware, what has opened your eyes to your role in writing your life?

> Love slays what we have been that we may be what we were not.
>
> —Saint Augustine

4. What is your response to Aunt Jane's statement that "there's a heap more in the cuttin' out and the sewin' than there is in the caliker"?[2]

5. Let all the group members read aloud their stories about family vacations or favorite pets. What did each story reveal to you about the teller? about the other characters? about family dynamics? about God?

Your Well of Stories

As you worked through the chapter, the questions may have reminded you of other scenes. Add these to your well of stories to write later. These scenes will form a working list that you will return to again and again.

chapter two

why write?

What began the change was the very writing itself. Let no one lightly set about such a work. Memory, once waked, will play the tyrant. I found I must set down (for I was speaking as before judges and must not lie) passions and thoughts of my own which I had clean forgotten. The past which I wrote down was not the past that I thought I had (all these years) been remembering. I did not, even when I had finished the book, see clearly many things that I see now. The change which writing wrought in me (and of which I did not write) was only a beginning; only to prepare me for the gods' surgery. They used my own pen to probe my wound.

—ORUAL, QUEEN OF GLOME,
in C. S. LEWIS, *Till We Have Faces*

We write to remember, learn, and understand. Writing forces us to think differently about the story, to choose and structure carefully what we tell. Like Orual in C. S. Lewis's retelling of the Psyche myth, *Till We Have Faces,* we will likely find that writing clarifies our memory. It exposes the places where we have downplayed either the harm done to us or what we really felt in the scene. Writing can also reveal where we have left an important character out of the story. Orual began her writing as a complaint against the gods for all the abuse and loneliness she had endured. She wrote what she knew, and the writing exposed another, deeper, truth. The writing revealed her own heart. We write because through writing we discover truth that we didn't know we knew. We write because one of the ways God speaks to us is through our stories.

> Living safely *is* dangerous.
> —Frederick Nietzsche, in Irvin Yalom,
> *When Nietzsche Wept*

According to church tradition, God reveals theological truth in four ways (called the Wesleyan quadrilateral): Scripture, reason, tradition, and experience. God seeks us through Scripture (divine, personal self-disclosure in specific historical events), through our reason (our natural instinct that there is a God), through tradition (what Christians across traditions and centuries have agreed on), and through our experience (conversion, answers to prayer, art, literature, relationships, nature, and our life narrative).

Another way to understand God's self-revelation is to divide it into two categories: special revelation is God's Word, and general revelation is everything else (nature, history, reason, tradition, and our experience). Either way, our experience plays an integral part in how we come to know God. He created us as beings who carry story, and our stories give us a glimpse of God.

The problem is that we so rarely tell our own stories. Stories surround us, but those stories are not ours. The statistics are hard to believe: people spend an incredible amount of time in front of the television set and surfing the Web compared to time spent together at the dinner table, talking with family members. This contrast speaks of parallel, busy, nonintersecting lives filled with sound bites and easy-to-digest video stories that we forget as soon as the screen goes blank. You don't have to be a Luddite to recognize the vaporous quality of the culture we have embraced. We choose to live vicariously through chat rooms or spectator sports or reality TV, while our stories lie dormant, left untold. The stories told on the television and the Internet and in fluff novels are not *our* stories. They neither ask anything of us nor tell us anything about ourselves. And perhaps that is their greatest draw. It is also their greatest drawback.

Sam Keen, an insightful writer on the subject of storytelling, says we are "a people written on from the outside."[1] When we abandoned the tribal fires and stopped telling our stories, we became blank slates waiting to be scribbled on by whomever happened to come along. In contrast, when we learn our stories and tell them, we write from the inside.

This is a book of storytelling, of writing from the inside. If that makes you uncomfortable, remember that your stories are only for you and for a select few listeners of your choosing. Protect your stories. Give them a place to grow without judging them. If the blank page intimidates you, write down pieces, phrases, bits of a story. Then link them together in sentences and later link the sentences into paragraphs.

A BIRD'S-EYE VIEW

Review chapter 1 in *To Be Told,* then read chapter 2, "What's Your Real Name?" The following questions invite you to take a bird's-eye view of your stories. Later, we will delve more deeply into each of these areas.

1. Who are the main characters in your story?

2. Who are the invisible characters (for example: a powerful ancestor, a family secret, money)?

3. List the most important settings in your life. These may include the home where you grew up, a vacation spot your family visited every year, or your junior high school. Describe two places from this list.

4. Draw a line graph of your life, showing peaks, valleys, and plateaus. Which stories correspond with the high points? the low points? the flat areas? Add these to your well of stories.

Although the process of naming children in most cultures no longer carries the same significance it did in ancient times, our names still reveal much about us.

5. Look up the meaning of your name in a name book or on the Internet. What personality traits does this meaning suggest? How does its meaning correspond with who you are? What aspects don't seem to fit you? If you have an untraditional name, what did your parents wish to communicate through its sound and meaning?

6. Why were you given your name? Were you, for instance, named after a relative, family friend, biblical character, athlete, or movie star?

7. What is the significance of your family name? Where did it originate?

8. What names have you been given (such as peacemaker, family hero, trouble-maker, slut, dumb jock, brain) that do not fit who you are?

Renaming is a common occurrence in the Bible. Abram ("exalted father") becomes Abraham ("father of many"). Sarai becomes Sarah. Jacob ("he deceives") becomes Israel ("he struggles with God") after a midnight wrestling match. Daniel becomes Belte-shazzar. In Isaiah 62, one of the signs of God's care, love, and honor for Zion is that it will be called by a new name.

> The nations will see your righteousness,
>   and all kings your glory;
> you will be called by a new name
>   that the mouth of the LORD will bestow.
> You will be a crown of splendor in the LORD's hand,
>   a royal diadem in the hand of your God.
> No longer will they call you Deserted,
>   or name your land Desolate.

But you will be called Hephzibah ["my delight is in her"],
> and your land Beulah ["married"];
for the LORD will take delight in you,
> and your land will be married.
As a young man marries a maiden,
> so will your sons marry you;
as a bridegroom rejoices over his bride,
> so will your God rejoice over you. (verses 2-5)

*9. Do you have an inkling of the name that God will one day give you? During dark nights of the soul, what do you fear your name will be? In the midst of buoyant hope, what do you wish your name might be?

WRITING VS. TELLING YOUR STORY

There is a significant difference between telling and writing our stories, though both are important. Told stories are more malleable, ephemeral, transitory. They exist, but not tangibly. As we're telling a story, we can judge our listeners' reactions and, in response, expand the story when they show interest and delete large portions when their attention wanders. We can also emphasize humor or tragedy depending on how the listeners respond. Because of this flexibility, told stories can more easily be dismissed as unimportant even when they are very important.

Writing has more substance and permanence. With written stories, we make a commitment to the text, and that commitment can be seen in the ink on paper. We have a written record. We leave a mark. Writing involves much more time and energy, and it requires us to consider words and how best to say what we want to express. Of the millions of details in any scene, for instance, we can include only a few. So writing forces us to reenter the scene and stand there awhile in order to choose the most powerful details. Because of this process, writing causes us to see differently. It brings everything into sharper relief. Writing also gives us the opportunity to tell our stories and then stand back and read them from a distance of time. When we write, we can listen to our own stories.

If you are doing this workbook with a story group, you will be reading your stories out loud. As with telling and writing, there is a significant difference between telling a story and reading what you wrote. It's fine to paraphrase your answers to the questions, but when it comes to your stories, it will be important to read what you wrote instead of telling an approximation of what you wrote.

Reading aloud will likely be a terrifying experience. Perhaps the only comfort is that it will be a similarly frightening experience for everyone else in the story group. After all, if we are intent on being honest, writing will uncover and reveal our stories in ways we can't control. Of course, we can use words to obfuscate the truth and muddy the waters, but that very action reveals that we are not willing to face something.

> No man is an island, entire of itself; every man is a piece of the continent, a part of the main. If a clod be washed away by the sea, Europe is the less, as well as if a promontory were, as well as if a manor of thy friend's or of thine own were: any man's death diminishes me, because I am involved in mankind, and therefore never send to know for whom the bell tolls; it tolls for thee.
>
> —JOHN DONNE, *Devotions Upon Emergent Occasions*

As you begin to write your stories, expect internal resistance: *This is stupid. I'm bored. I have more important things to do. This doesn't make sense. My writing is not deep enough.* Then go ahead and read your stories anyway.

One purpose of being in a story group or choosing a friend to whom you can read your stories is to provide you with safe listeners who can see into your stories in a way you can't. When you read your stories aloud, you are stuck with your words. Even if you begin to fear you've lost your audience, you still have just your words. Reading your story exactly as you wrote it serves several purposes. It forces you to write more carefully, to choose the words and phrases that best describe the characters, setting, and action. Reading also helps your listeners observe what parts of your story affect you most—where your voice catches, where your tone changes. And it gives you the opportunity for specific feedback. Your listener might say: "I was confused at this part" or "Why do you think you used that particular word?" You can then use the feedback as you rework the story.

Writing vs. Journaling or Reporting Your Story

Writing your stories is different from both journaling and reporting. Journaling tends to be stream-of-conscience, feelings-based, informal writing. Reporting records facts in a detached manner, answering who, what, when, where, why, how. Both have value, but neither has the potential for healing that they have when employed together. By integrating them into your storytelling, you experience the whole story instead of just part.

> I've got these tears from a long time ago. / I need to cry thirty years or so.
> —John Hiatt, "Thirty Years of Tears," *Stolen Moments* CD

Also, with journaling, since you write purely for yourself, you can skip parts and jump to conclusions. As you write your stories, assume that your audience doesn't know you. Assume that they have never been to your house or met your family. Include enough detail to give them a feel for both the people and the places in your story.

10. Go back to your well of stories. Choose a scene that contains strong emotion and write it like a newspaper article. From a removed stance, give just the facts.

11. Now rewrite the scene and tell only the emotions. Don't mention events. Instead tell how you felt about those events. Looking over the following list of emotions might be helpful. In your writing, try to capture how you experience these emotions physically in your body.

calm	undecided	grieving	poisonous
blissful	thoughtful	guilty	impotent
happy	withdrawn	paranoid	betrayed
joyful	puzzled	regretful	critical
optimistic	sheepish	harassed	angry
satisfied	confused	exhausted	jealous
curious	shy	apologetic	prudish
smug	bored	disappointed	suspicious
lovestruck	embarrassed	cautious	dangerous
confident	reserved	worried	skeptical
ecstatic	protective	helpless	obstinate
arrogant	distant	horrified	furious
sympathetic	fearful	scared	aggressive
innocent	ambivalent	hopeless	envious
interested	hurt	surprised	irritated
tender	anxious	hysterical	determined
playful	miserable	disgusted	
relieved	lonely	shocked	
indifferent	sad	frightened	

*12. How do the two tellings of your story (strictly factual versus feelings-oriented) differ? Rewrite that story (or, if you prefer, another story) and integrate both facts and emotions.

OVERCOMING RESISTANCE

I (Lisa) recently e-mailed Selby, a writer friend, telling him I hadn't been writing.

I have started writing, if it can be called that. Really it is more like staring into the middle distance with my fingers poised over the keyboard. I have followed the first rule of writing: apply posterior to chair. But the writing part still eludes me. Sometimes a deadline is the only thing that can bring words to life.

As I struggled to write the introduction to this workbook, my hands trembled and my heart raced. I have loved words and reading all my life, but putting my own words on paper terrifies me. Not always, obviously, since I have made my living as an editor and writer, but the terror comes just at the point when the words matter the most to me. Then I start hearing those relentless voices: family members who believe it is destructive to revisit the past; an acquaintance who will pull out a passage and make fun of it; me, who questions what I could possibly offer when I don't have things all figured out myself. Perhaps we can be partners in misery as we write. It might even be fun to have corporate fits of doubt and despair.

For many people, writing doesn't begin until after the trash has been taken out, the desk straightened, important phone calls made, the bathroom cleaned, and teeth checked in the mirror. A lot of work is accomplished in the effort to avoid the work of writing. Novelist William Faulkner once said, "I don't believe the good people of Mississippi ever will understand how a man can sit in the shade and make $30,000 for defacing a few scraps of paper (the Nobel Prize paid that amount). In Mississippi the people work for their money and you can understand how they feel about writing, why it puzzles them."[2] What Faulkner's fellow Mississippians didn't understand was just how much work writing actually is, just how many obstacles most people have to overcome in order to deface a few scraps of paper. Writing is hard labor, but the labor is almost entirely internal.

In the interest of productive paper defacing, I offer these suggestions:

Create a sacred space for writing. Find time when you can be alone, even if that means being alone in a crowd of people. Clear a small area of distractions. Use your favorite pen. Make a cup of tea. Put a bit of Belgian chocolate on a china plate. Light candles. Listen to instrumental music. Offer yourself bits of comfort as you engage in the labor of writing, but don't let preparations consume your writing time.

Write even when you don't have anything to say. Sometimes you have to prime the pump by writing even when you don't know what to write. Often, through the act of writing, we discover that we have more to say than we thought we did. So start with a word or a phrase and then add another word or phrase and see where they lead you. Write whatever comes to mind. If it's a grocery list, write it down, then put it aside. You may first need to clear your mind of distractions and clutter before you can begin the real writing.

> In hell, nothing connects with nothing.
> —T. S. ELIOT, quoted in *A World of Ideas*

Start small. The Mississippi River is the Mississippi River whether you are looking at it where it starts as a trickle of water in Minnesota or where it finally merges with the Gulf of Mexico in a massive river delta. With that truth in mind, start your story where you can walk across instead of where you must take a ferry. Choose a scene that lasted only a couple of minutes and tell it well. Focus on one interaction from your birthday party when you were seven or on what your father said to you after the bully at school beat you up. Then expand the scene or move on to another scene. If you try to tell your whole life in one story, you will never make it across that river.

Beware the critics who will plague you. For some reason writing brings out more critics than most other activities. They stand around like phantoms, gazing over your shoulder and offering commentary: "You can't even spell," "What schlock. Why are you even trying to write?" and "*That* sounds *really* stupid." After I told a friend about all my critics, she said, "There sure are a lot of people writing with you." Dump the critics. Lock them in a dark closet. Or threaten them: *If you don't evaporate, I'm going to write an unflattering story about you.*

Assume a compassionate, interested audience. Once you've dispatched the critics, you can assume that your audience has also wrestled with words and has an appreciation for your labor. Your audience doesn't care about things like spelling and punctuation. Instead, they are drawn to vivid scenes and well-drawn characters.

Show; don't tell. This mantra of writing is overused but underemployed. Writing that engages us reveals; it doesn't merely tell. So instead of saying that your best friend was furious with you, show this by describing the friend's squinty eyes, red face, and tight mouth. Give bits of terse dialogue. Think back to why you knew your friend was angry and put these clues in the story. Instead of saying that your brother is reckless, describe how he switches lanes on the freeway and how he jaywalks on busy city streets.

> To be a person is to have a story to tell.
> —ISAK DINESEN

Integrate emotions and facts. Write both what happened and what you felt about what happened. Reread your story to see if you can place yourself in the scene. Does the story make clear where you are physically in the scene? Does it show what you were feeling?

Take risks in what you write. In addition to the easy stories, tackle some that frighten you, that don't have a satisfying ending, or that seem out of character for you.

Expect feelings of futility and emptiness. Writing, like anything that really matters, rarely offers instant or repeated gratification. You will probably think, *Why bother?* as you deal with words that don't work together and stories that seem to go nowhere. Like any other journey, writing sometimes requires a bit of plodding in order to reach a place with a stunning view.

FOR DISCUSSION IN YOUR STORY GROUP—MEETING 2

Reading a story from one's life aloud to a group can be terrifying. Afterward the reader will likely feel exposed and vulnerable. So feedback should be gentle. At the same time, overly positive feedback won't be helpful.

Here are a few questions to keep in mind as you listen to the stories of others:

- Are you able to see the scene? Could you draw a picture of the setting?
- Can you picture the characters? What do you learn about the characters? Is anyone missing from the scene?
- How did you feel in response to the story? What emotion did the writer capture well?
- What holes exist in the story? Where did the writer leave out important details?
- What do you think it was like to be the person in that situation? What do you feel on her or his behalf?
- What does the story stir up in you? In what ways does it remind you of your own story?

Read aloud Orual's words quoted at the beginning of this chapter.

1. What do you see more clearly in your story as a result of the writing you've done so far? Did you write any of your stories differently than you have told them in the past?
2. Describe your feelings as you wrote your story. What is it like to see the story in ink on a page?
3. What do you feel about the prospect of reading your stories to a group?

4. How was the process of writing a story different from telling it?
5. Let each person read his or her story aloud to the group. After each person reads, allow time for feedback from others.

YOUR WELL OF STORIES

As you worked through the chapter, the questions may have reminded you of other scenes. Add these to your well of stories to write later.

chapter three

family stories

Old man Falls roared: "Cunnel was settin' thar in a cheer, his sock feet propped on the po'ch railin', smokin' this hyer very pipe. Old Louvinia was settin' on the steps, shellin' a bowl of peas fer supper. And a feller was glad to git even peas sometimes, in them days. And you was settin' back agin' the post. They wa'nt nobody else thar 'cep' yo' aunt, the one 'fo' Miss Jenny come. Cunnel had sont them two gals to Memphis to yo' gran'pappy when he fust went away. You was 'bout half-grown, I reckon. How old was you then, Bayard?"

"Fourteen," old Bayard answered.

"Hey?"

"Fourteen," Bayard shouted. "Do I have to tell you that every time you tell me this d— story?"

"And thar you all was a-settin'," old man Falls continued, unruffled, "when they turned in at the gate and come trottin' up the carriage drive."

—WILLIAM FAULKNER, *Flags in the Dust*

Stories have enormous potential to shape our lives. Some of the most powerful are stories about a family told within that family, stories that are repeated over years and generations. In other words, the stories that are unique to each of us. Because they reveal where we came from and who we are both corporately and individually, family stories are the most valuable part of our inheritance.

Just as old man Falls brings Colonel Sartoris into the room through his oft-repeated tale, our family stories impact us whether we're aware of it or not. In William Faulkner's novel, old man Falls tells how Colonel John Sartoris outwitted the Yankees who had come to arrest him. Sartoris sat on the porch gawking and told them that John Sartoris lived "down the road a piece" but that he was off fighting the Yanks again. When the Yankee soldiers demanded that he accompany them, Sartoris limped into the house to get his boots and, as soon as he was out of their sight, ran to the creek where Bayard stood waiting with his stallion. As Sartoris rode away, he instructed Bayard to tell his aunt that he wouldn't be home for supper.[1]

> You *are* your stories. You are the product of all the stories you have heard and lived—and many that you have never heard. They have shaped how you see yourself, the world, and your place in it…. Stories link past, present, and future in a way that tells us where we have been (even before we were born), where we are, and where we could be going.
>
> —Daniel Taylor, *Tell Me a Story*

John Sartoris's descendants and the rest of the town live in the shadow of his legend. Even after his death, he is present through stories and revered as the pinnacle of Southern manliness. Bayard and others carry the weight of the gilded stories about Colonel Sartoris, unable to live up to the myth.

Often fiction captures the truth better than nonfiction. Later in this workbook we'll look at ways to use the elements of fiction (character, setting, dialogue, plot) to better write our own true stories.

1. Look at this chapter's opening scene from Faulkner's *Flags in the Dust*. What do you learn about old man Falls from this short interaction? Notice how a couple of key words such as *roared* and *unruffled* clue you in to his character. What do you think would happen if someone interrupted his story? Example: *Old man Falls tells this story more for himself than for his audience.*

2. Write down some of the distinct words, accents, and repeated phrases or aphorisms used in your family. You will use these later as a resource to help you better capture the characters in your stories.

FAMILY STORIES THAT CREATE

Family stories reveal who we are and where we've come from. They tell us what is important in our culture and clan and how we fit into a certain group that is related by genetics, marriage, and adoption. The best stories create a sense of hope and joy at the strength, courage, tenderness, quirkiness, and other characteristics that God uniquely created each family to reveal. The very best stories remind us of our ability to shape our lives and make meaning. Read the section "In the Name of the Father and Mother" in chapter 2 of *To Be Told*.

Stories Give Us a Sense of Belonging

Like our physical traits, our stories brand us as part of a particular family. Unlike physical traits, stories cross boundaries, impacting us whether our relationship is by genetics, adoption, or marriage. We are participants in and heirs to our family stories. At the most basic level, the fact that we are characters, or related to characters, in the stories confirms our existence. Beyond that, family stories can affirm and define personal relationships and create emotional bonds of a shared history.[2] In Eileen Silva Kindig's *Remember the Time…? The Power and Promise of Family Storytelling,* she says that family stories "illustrate all the glorious, crazy, eccentric, touching, wonderful ways that your family is different from every other family."[3] These stories, Kindig points out, also remind us of our spiritual connections with families everywhere.

Family stories weave a web around us and give us people with whom we can say, "Remember when…?" This web can sustain us or entrap us. Either way, the stories wield great influence. Elizabeth Stone has written, "Even if we loathe our families, in order to know ourselves, we seem to need to know about them, just as prologue. Not to know is to live with some of the disorientation and anxiety of the amnesiac."[4] Without stories we are adrift. Without stories we have no pasts.

Stories Socialize Us and Encode the Rules of the Family

Faced with his daughter's crying over math homework, Mike tells her a story of how he struggled to understand geometry and, after much labor, finally got it. Through his story, Mike instills the importance of perseverance in his family. As a teenager, Jason tells his younger brother about when he broke his leg but didn't cry, explaining how their family defines strength and courage in boys. Families use stories to establish the family culture: values, gender identity and biases, expected behavior, and how to make decisions.[5] Certain stories survive and are retold because they are touchstones. They reveal what is true, or what the family needs to be true, or what the family wishes were true.

Stories Encapsulate the Essence of a Family

Stories explain and buttress the definition the family has of itself. Family legends (those stories repeatedly told) tell us what sort of stock we come from and what we value. David Kennedy, one of Robert F. Kennedy's sons, was not viewed by some people as truly a part of the family because he did not have the aggressiveness considered an essential Kennedy trait. Whether factually true or not, family legends distill how a family defines itself. And each legend contains myriad smaller stories.

Stories Help Us Understand Who We Are
and Why We Do Certain Things

Stories reveal character traits, opinions, biases, and fears that have been handed down unwittingly through generations. When she was twenty, Cory refused an operation that she desperately needed. In her family there was a history of hostility toward doctors. Although the stories behind that hostility had rarely been told, Cory picked up on the family ethos and enacted it in her own life.

In a more direct way, our families mirror back to us who we are through the stories they tell about us, and often we later demonstrate those traits. So which is it? Do the stories create who we are or merely reflect who we are? The answer is probably both. By telling our own stories, we begin to understand what we have experienced, so that we can then learn from those experiences about who we are.

> Die at the right time.... Live when you live! Death loses its terror if one dies when one has consummated one's life.... Have you lived your life? Or been lived by it? Chosen it? Or did it choose you? Loved it? Or regretted it?... [Are you standing] by helplessly, grieving for the life you never lived?
>
> —FREDERICK NIETZSCHE, in Irvin Yalom, *When Nietzsche Wept*

Stories Remind Us of Our Ability to Shape and Create

Sarah, normally cautious and practical, gave up everything to follow a dream of getting a graduate degree in art, and she ended up loving the career that resulted. When faced with another huge decision, she looked back at that story and reminded herself that taking great risks can result in a richer life. Stories help us recall times when things looked dodgy but we made it through anyhow. Such stories give us courage to face new challenges and to find new patterns by which to make sense of our lives. Life becomes more meaningful when we understand that we create our stories as much as we are created by them.

Stories Make Meaning

Stories help us figure things out. By understanding them, we can begin to see some of the brushstrokes of the Great Artist. Author and professor Daniel Taylor writes:

> The least livable life is the one without coherence—nothing connects, nothing means anything. Stories make connections. They allow us to see our past, our present, and our future as interrelated and purposeful.... The stories we value most reassure us that life is worth the pain, that meaning is not an illusion, and that others share our experience with us.[6]

Stories Are Life

Through stories we live our lives over and over: the hilarity, grief, overcoming of obstacles, joy, anger, reconciliation, foolish choices, healing, struggle, crazy coincidences, pain, and love. Christa's family laughs at their insane dog, Ginger, who stole anything the neighbors left outdoors. Ginger's kleptomania disrupted the quiet and respectable life of Christa's family, but now they find great amusement in the stories. Amanda's family tells of when she beat up the school bully to protect her younger brother. Teri's friends tell of the time when a car hit her while she was riding her bike. Doctors told her she would never walk again, but she proved them wrong. Stories like these serve as our record of the complexity of being human.

As you answer the questions below, it may help to look through old photos of your family to stir your memory.

3. List some outstanding physical characteristics and personality traits of your family.

*4. What are your family's foundational stories? In other words, what stories tell you who you are as a family, your family characteristics, and the rules by which you live?

5. Write a paragraph about the sort of stock you come from—Scandinavian, pioneer, fundamentalist, seafaring, adventuresome, risk-avoidant.

6. What are your family legends, such as how your grandparents met when she coyly offered him a bite of apple or the loony things your uncle did when he was drunk?

7. What stories are most frequently told in your family? What stories get told at reunions and holidays?

8. What stories are rarely or never told? When you were growing up, what stories were avoided or marginalized? Add these and the stories above to your well of stories.

Family Stories That Destroy

In the scene from *Flags in the Dust* that opened this chapter, the now-old Bayard and his descendants live under the weight of Colonel Sartoris's glamorous and idealized escapades. The family steadily declines after the colonel dies, surviving by living off the glory of the past.

Like old man Falls, Aunt Jenny tells family stories, one in particular about John Sartoris's brother and his friend.

> As she grew older the tale itself grew richer and richer, taking on a mellow splendor like wine; until what had been a hair-brained prank of two heedless and reckless boys wild with their own youth, was become a gallant and finely tragical focal-point to which the history of the race had been raised from out the old miasmic swamps of spiritual sloth by two angels valiantly and glamorously fallen and strayed, altering the course of human events and purging the souls of men.[7]

Family stories take on a life of their own and, whether they are true or false, become truth for the family. These stories create a sense of belonging and identity, but they also can be toxic. What can be used to create also can be used to destroy. Because of this, we are wise to study how our stories can harm us.

We Can Refuse to Create Our Own Stories

Our stories are like air: we rarely notice them because they are what we have always known. That's why, as children, we view our own families as the norm. In Jessa's family, for instance, no one mentioned the fact that her mother drank too much. Jessa made dinner and got her younger siblings ready for bed while her mother slept. She simply accepted that, as the oldest, she had to look after everyone else. Jessa was her family's caregiver and rescuer. Only after she married did she begin to question that role.

Often we don't even notice our stories until we reach our thirties. During that decade of life, many people start seeing a counselor because they realize they have been living out a story they didn't write. This discovery leads some on a journey of learning to tell their own stories. Others see an insurmountable mountain and turn back. *Why would I choose the deprivations of struggling up the mountain,* they ask, *when I could enjoy an easier life down here in the valley?*

But we begin to die when we accept certain definitions and stories of ourselves simply because that's who we have always been told we are. We become less gloriously human when we say "That's just the way it is" as an excuse not to change or explore other possibilities or hope for more. God invites us to take the materials he has given us and rewrite the story to make it uniquely ours. As Salman Rushdie observed, "Those who do not have the power over the story that dominates their lives, power to retell it, rethink it, deconstruct it, joke about it, and change it as times change, truly are power-less, because they cannot think new thoughts."[8]

We Can Deceive Ourselves with Stories

Sometimes a family grasps its legends so tightly that even if the stories are found to be inaccurate, they still are accepted. To correct the falsehoods would require family members to shift their images of themselves and the family. This reluctance to disrupt the equilibrium of the family system can also be seen in the blindness we have to our personal stories.[9]

Angela's father sexually abused her, but because he also favored her as his little princess, she chose to ignore the impact of the abuse. To address it would require her to reevaluate their relationship and lose her status as his favorite. Angela chose instead to blame her distant and critical mother for the problems in the family and thereby keep intact her role as her father's princess.

To protect ourselves from the implications of embracing the truth of a disturbing story, we gloss over inconsistencies and leap over gaps in logic. We either tell sanitized versions of our life stories, leaving out shameful behavior or harm that we can't bear to face, or we make a joke

> We laugh uproariously, embellish our favorite tales, interrupt each other and argue hotly over details. Though there are only four of us, the room is so crowded that the cast of characters spills out into the foyer and crams the kitchen.... It is one big multicultural, intergenerational, three-dimensional bash.
> —EILEEN KINDIG, talking about family story-telling night in *Remember the Time...?*

out of it. We carefully choose our heroes and villains so they do not disrupt the status quo.[10] Then we protect these stories by surrounding ourselves with others who believe, or at least won't question, the myth.

We Can Use Stories to Protect Ourselves by Harming Others

A study of Kurdish masculine identity examined the coming-of-age rituals of Kurdish men. As children, the boys spend all their time with the women of the family and become very attached to their mothers. When it's time for the boys to enter the world of men, their fathers dissolve this attachment to the women by telling them "horrific stories of [women's] perfidy and dishonor."[11] These family tales of women's betraying and dishonoring men have created a culture that fears, exploits, and subjugates women.

> Our meanings are almost always inseparable from stories, in all realms of life. And, once again, family stories, invisible as air, weightless as dreams, are there for us. To make our own meanings out of our myriad stories is to achieve balance—at once a way to be part of and apart from our families, a way of holding on and letting go.
>
> —ELIZABETH STONE, *Black Sheep and Kissing Cousins*

Similarly, the history of the United States is rife with stories of how each successive wave of immigrants became the lowest segment of society and the butt of jokes told by those who had happened to arrive in the United States a few years earlier. We also categorize and demean others by telling stories about nerdy computer geeks or obtuse jocks. We repeat flawed assumptions that people from certain ethnicities are lazy and dimwitted and that others are arrogant and blind to the plight of everyone else. We make sarcastic comments about gender, politics, race, and religion. Through these remarks that tear down the character, beliefs, and convictions of others, we bolster ourselves.

We Can Silence Stories

Stories that are left untold can be just as powerful as told stories, and the unspoken ones are more dangerous because they are unacknowledged. Story researchers tell of people who never revealed terrible tragedies they experienced, yet those tragedies were repeated by their children. The silent story holds so much power that other family members unconsciously pick up on it and reenact it.[12] Joe Eszterhas, Hollywood screenwriter for movies such as *Flashdance, Jagged Edge,* and *Basic Instinct,* also wrote *Music Box,* an anguished film about an American woman who learns that her father was a Nazi. Eszterhas later found out that during the Nazi occupation of Hungary, his father had written a highly anti-Semitic book.[13]

Silenced stories also create a subterranean text to relationships where meaning becomes ambiguous and secret alliances and coalitions exist.[14] Recently I (Lisa) blindly walked into a social situation that had a subterranean text. A friend of mine expressed a need for legal advice, so I recommended another friend who is a lawyer, and he eagerly wrote down her name. Later, I saw the lawyer and told her I had recommended her to a friend. When she found out who it was, she said, "I would never even allow that man in my office." Apparently she had heard something about him that she didn't like, and when she walked away, I felt as though I had done something wrong but wasn't sure what it could be. Things did not make sense, and what had started out pleasantly suddenly took on dark, dangerous overtones. In the middle of it all, this image popped into my mind:

> I am pedaling a tricycle down a sidewalk past carefully groomed, corduroy
> lawns. Dads jog behind jogging strollers. Across the street, a sprinkler waters
> the lawn and sidewalk as it makes its ch-ch-ch-ch semicircles. Children playing
> tag shriek in delight as they evade "it." I close my eyes for a moment and find
> myself in the middle of a street riddled with potholes and littered with discarded
> syringes. Drug dealers offer crack, and gang members break the last panes of
> glass in the deserted, graffiti-covered buildings. Prostitutes advertise their wares.
> Sordid groups of grimy, T-shirted men clot on street corners, then disperse and
> clot again around a loner. They push him around then pound him with their
> fists and leave him in a crumpled mass on the pavement. I pedal very slowly
> hoping that no one will notice me.

We Can Allow Stories to Become Rigid

We often resort to using story skeletons, the shortcuts and generalizations that make our stories more coherent and understandable.[15] For example, a woman contemplating divorce might structure her story along the lines of "he just can't detach himself from his mother, which makes him a terrible husband." This common skeleton makes sense out of myriad factors but ignores other crucial elements of the story line. (In this story, for example, the woman ignores her own role in the breakdown of her marriage.)

Some predictable skeleton stories in families include love at first sight, the family scapegoat, the lost fortune, the sacred son, the martyr-parent, and the forgotten daughter. These stories assign family members certain roles not because of who the players are, but because of whom the family needs them to be.[16] Defining one person as the bad one or the sickly one or the one who always needs help makes the other family members feel better about themselves and maintains family equilibrium. Assigning one child the role of family hero relieves everyone else from having to be perfect. Roles cause us to focus the spotlight on a few actors while the other characters in the story remain hidden in the wings. By focusing on certain roles, families can conveniently ignore all the other family dynamics.

*9. Write a story that your family has used to protect itself by harming others. What does this reveal about your family's beliefs?

10. What stories does your family need to be true? Which stories does your family wish were true?

11. What are your family's subterranean texts? You may not know the story behind them, but in what circumstances have you felt as if you just pedaled your tricycle into a war zone?

12. List the skeleton stories in your family. Choose one and write a couple of paragraphs about it.

13. What are the stories told about you that do not accurately reflect who you are?

14. Who tells these stories? Why?

15. What stories do you most frequently tell about other members of your family?

16. Are these stories true?

Stories in my (Lisa's) family are nearly nonexistent, which is probably what has made them so irresistible to me. I have spent countless hours creating photo albums both for myself and my family. I interviewed my grandparents about their lives. I have written down tales of the daily life of my niece and nephew. I am fascinated by genealogy. Others view me with some amusement and, at times, fear. But the stories have called to me. They have whispered that I was living out of a script that had been handed down to me, and I wanted to understand that script to see if I could change some lines.

17. Write a family story, untold or untrue, that has impacted your life.

*18. Think through archetypes such as the scapegoat, black sheep, hero, princess, clown, martyr, troublemaker, and sacrificial lamb. Who in your family falls into these categories? Tell a couple of their stories.

19. Pick a phrase from your answers to question 2 earlier in this chapter and write one of the scenes where the phrase was used.

20. Notice that in the scene at the beginning of this chapter, old man Falls wasn't present when the Yankees rode up to the house of Colonel Sartoris. Why, then, does he tell the story? Why do you think Bayard is not the storyteller? What stories do others tell about your family?

FOR DISCUSSION IN YOUR STORY GROUP—MEETING 3

For most people, family stories are sacred ground. They reside near the core of who we are. So even if a storyteller identifies a particular story as false, she or he is likely still struggling with the implications of this for daily life and family relationships. Keep the sacredness of these stories in mind as group members read aloud one of their own. Be gentle with one another. Be zealous about confidentiality. And take off your shoes. You are on holy ground.

1. What is the truest story that your family tells?

2. What are some of the worn-out aphorisms used by your family? In what contexts are they used?

3. Discuss your answers to question 10: What stories does your family need to be true? Which stories does your family wish were true?

4. Have each person in the group choose one of the family stories she or he wrote and read it aloud. What roles do you see enacted in one another's stories? What does each story tell you about the family? Who is missing from the story?

Your Well of Stories

As you worked through the chapter, the questions may have reminded you of other scenes. Add these to your well of stories to write later.

chapter four

how truthful is memory?

It's time to be blunt.

I'm forty-three years old, true, and I'm a writer now, and a long time ago I walked through Quang Ngai Province as a foot soldier.

Almost everything else is invented.

But it's not a game. It's a form. Right here, now, as I invent myself, I'm thinking of all I want to tell you about why this book is written as it is. For instance, I want to tell you this: twenty years ago I watched a man die on a trail near the village of My Khe. I did not kill him. But I was present, you see, and my presence was guilt enough. I remember his face, which was not a pretty face, because his jaw was in his throat, and I remember feeling the burden of responsibility and grief. I blamed myself. And rightly so, because I was present.

But listen. Even that story is made up.

I want you to feel what I felt. I want you to know why story-truth is truer sometimes than happening-truth.

Here is the happening-truth. I was once a soldier. There were many bodies, real bodies with real faces, but I was young then and I was afraid to look. And now, twenty years later, I'm left with faceless responsibility and faceless grief.

> Here is the story-truth. He was a slim, dead, almost dainty young
> man of about twenty. He lay in the center of a red clay trail near the
> village of My Khe. His jaw was in his throat. His one eye was shut, the
> other eye was a star-shaped hole. I killed him.
>
> —TIM O'BRIEN, *The Things They Carried*

What makes a story true? Is it less true if it has been embroidered? Is it more true if it's told fact-by-fact exactly as it happened? In *The Things They Carried,* a novel about the war in Vietnam, Tim O'Brien explores the nature of truth and storytelling through the stories of several characters. In the passage quoted above, the narrator explains the difference between factual truth and visceral truth: he didn't kill the young man, but it better explains his ragged emotions to say that he did.

MEMORY AND TRUTH

Our stories give our lives structure and meaning. The word *story* shares the same root as *history.* Both root us to a time and place and heritage. But our stories are not, strictly speaking, history. They are our history as we remember it. They are facts, impressions, and emotions, all filtered through the rest of our life stories. Which is not to say that what we remember did not happen the way we remember it. It's to point out that memory is somewhat fluid and that to arrive at the actual, fact-by-fact, definitive truth that everyone agrees on is nearly impossible, as any historian or lawyer or police officer at the scene of an accident will attest.[1]

> Of course you suffer, it's the price
> of vision. Of course you are fearful,
> living *means* to be in danger. Grow
> hard!
>
> —FREDERICK NIETZSCHE, in Irvin Yalom,
> *When Nietzsche Wept*

A friend of mine (Lisa) refers to his memory as a Labrador retriever. He sends it to fetch something and off it lopes, sniffing around and poking its wet nose into odd corners. Eventually it comes back, tail wagging happily, with what it found. What his memory returns with may not be the same as what someone else's memory retrieves even if they both find the same event.

As you write your stories, you're writing the truth as you know it, not the truth as your father or your neighbor or your cousin knows it. You're writing the emotional truth, not necessarily the factual truth. The latter often misses the point. The truth about your grandfather may be that he worked long hours to provide for his family. The truth may also be that by demanding absolute, immediate obedience from his children, he made them pay for his exhaustion. The truth may be that you excelled in sports because you enjoyed playing the game. It may also be that you were driven by the fear of failing at something that was so important to your parents.

In her book *Writing Fiction,* Janet Burroway notes:

> There is a curious prejudice built into our language that makes us speak of telling *the* truth but telling *a* lie. No one supposes that all conceivable falsehood can be wrapped up in a single statement called 'the lie'; lies are manifold, varied, and specific. But truth is supposed to be absolute: the truth, the whole truth, and nothing but the truth. This is, of course, impossible nonsense, and *telling a lie* is a truer phrase than *telling the truth.* Fiction does not have to tell *the* truth, but *a* truth.[2]

In the same way, your stories will never fully capture the definitive truth. What you strive for is to tell *a* truth. Think of your writing not as a photograph but as an impressionistic painting. You endeavor to capture a truth underneath the facts.

Writing emotional truth is not a blank check to claim as truth anything you wish were true. Instead, it's a way to get at the deeper truth, what Tim O'Brien calls the story-truth, not the happening-truth. You can't use emotional truth in a court of law or to win an argument. But you can use it to reveal to yourself truths that you didn't know you knew.

If this issue of telling emotional truth makes you uneasy, remember that you don't have to defend your stories or let others read them. Write your stories, then let them steep for a while. Later go back and see if they still tell the truth. You might find that they are not quite truthful enough, that you did not fully explore the deepest truth in them.

As I (Lisa) work with people to help them write their stories, I often hear: "But I don't remember exactly what happened." Their writing stalls because they don't recall details. Where memory is foggy, deduce what likely happened. You may not remember the exact words of an argument with your father, but you can come up with what probably was said. Similarly, use your general knowledge of elementary-school restrooms to infer what the restroom looked like when you were in third grade and the bigger kids tried to put your head in the toilet. In my experience, once people realize that they are free to make up what was likely the truth, they begin to remember details they thought they had forgotten. Without the pressure of having to be factually precise, the Labrador tends to retrieve the right items and then eagerly go out again to search for more.

*1. Look again at the narrator's two versions of the truth in the passage from *The Things They Carried*. What are the differences? In your opinion, is "story-truth" a valid truth? Why or why not? And if not, how could you make up for the insufficiencies of "happening-truth"?

*2. Choose a scene from your well of stories and write the factual truth.

*3. Now write the emotional truth of the same story.

4. Compare the two versions of your story. What are the differences and similarities?

Sometimes what the Labrador of your memory retrieves is not what you requested. Sometimes he returns with an odd fragment, and only later do you realize the connection between what was sought and what was retrieved. When the Lab happily offers you a filthy, shapeless object that you're reluctant to touch, tell him "Good boy!" even if you don't mean it. Then send him off to get something else so you'll have time to examine his find. Pick it up between two fingers and hold it at arm's length. Sniff, but don't take a big whiff or you may be sorry. Turn it around. Feel the weight. If you still don't know what it is, put it down and study it from a distance. Poke it with a stick. Then write about what you see. As you write, you may figure out what it is.

A woman with whom I (Lisa) work suffered severe emotional abuse at the hands of her parents. "Caroline" told me a story that she couldn't get out of her head. The strange thing was that in this story "nothing happened." Caroline didn't see any point in writing it, but she did anyway—and the story surprised her with what it revealed. The plot was simple: Caroline and her sister Lizzy were playing outside in the swimming pool, and their uncle came and told Lizzy to come inside the house. End of story. Or, more accurately, end of the facts. But it was only the beginning of the emotional truth.

As Caroline wrote, she realized that the story represented a pattern in her life. In this tormented family where love was nearly nonexistent, any perversion of love was better than none at all. Lizzy was the favorite, and though their uncle sexually abused her, she had a position of power in the family. Caroline lived constantly in her sister's shadow as the one not chosen by her uncle or by anyone else. The story revealed

> Absolute occurrence is irrelevant. A thing may happen and be a total lie; another thing may not happen and be truer than the truth.
>
> —Tim O'Brien, *The Things They Carried*

Caroline's ambivalence: she did not want the abuse, but she hungered for the attention. In this story where nothing happened, much happened.

The most problematic stories frequently offer the richest rewards. There is a reason why they're ornery, why the words won't flow and the sentences come out wrinkled and wailing like a newborn. Telling true stories is a birthing process, and it requires painful labor.

5. List some scenes from your life when "nothing" happened.

Read chapter 3, "What Makes a Good Story?" in *To Be Told*. A good story contains certain narrative elements that work together to make the story both engaging and revelatory.

In *The Things They Carried*, the men in Alpha Company view stories in very different ways. These men reflect some common attitudes toward stories, and their beliefs about what makes up a good tale affect the way they tell their stories. Rat Kiley, who wants his listeners to feel what he felt, has a fluid theory of what is factual. Mitchell Sanders appreciates a good story but expects a neat ending complete with a moral and a clear sense of good and bad. Norman Bowker is struggling to reconcile the horror of his war stories with his present life. He wants to tell his stories, but he can't find people who will listen. Tim, the narrator, has found some healing through telling his stories.

> War stories, like any good story, are finally about the human heart. About the choices we make, or fail to make. The forfeitures in our lives. Stories are to console and to inspire and to help us heal.
>
> —Tim O'Brien, in the lecture "Writing Vietnam"

Some of the ways people define a good story are: *It has a riveting plot. It struggles with the human condition and matters of the heart. It's a quick, light read. It captures the nuances of speech. It is complex and thought provoking. It's upbeat and makes me feel hopeful about the world. The characters are fully developed and very human. It looks unflinchingly at life. The descriptions are evocative. It makes me see things differently. It is logical and easy to follow. It's funny. It has a satisfying ending with no loose ends. It challenges me to reconsider what I believe. It is entertaining and doesn't require much of me. It allows me to see life through the eyes of someone else.*

6. What are your favorite novels and short stories? What characteristics do they have in common?

7. How do you define a good story?

As you write, be aware of how your definition of a good story shapes your writing. For example, if you prefer stories that end neatly with a moral or you only enjoy happy stories, you will tend to write stories in the same way. Guard against recreating the truth to fit a certain structure, style, or genre of storytelling. Write the story as you remember it and as you feel it, regardless of the shape it takes.

COLLECTING STONES FROM THE JORDAN RIVER

A good friend recently encouraged me (Lisa) to write down some of my painful stories. I resisted. "What's the point?" I asked. He laughed. We both knew I was working on this workbook and that I had just voiced the same question many readers will be asking themselves: *I'm busy, and writing stories takes time and emotional energy. What will I have when I finish? Will it be worth all the pain and effort?*

Considering the reasons we write might help answer those questions. We write to pass on our stories to our children, and we write so we have a record for when cataracts form on our memory. We write because our stories remind us of our ability to shape and create. We write because we hope to see our suffering redeemed, to see that in God's economy nothing is wasted. But most of all we write for the sake of our relationship with God. We write ultimately because it reveals not only our heart toward God, our patterns of sabotage, and our self-protective style of relating, but also the hand of a good God in our lives and his outrageous offer to let us cowrite with him. And we write because God commands us to remember.

> God acts in history and in your and my brief histories not as the puppeteer who sets the scene and works the strings but rather as the great director who no matter what role fate casts us in conveys to us somehow from the wings, if we have our eyes, ears, hearts open and sometimes even if we don't, how we can play those roles in a way to enrich and ennoble and hallow the whole vast drama of things including our own small but crucial parts in it.
>
> —FREDERICK BUECHNER, *Telling Secrets*

In Hebrew the word *zakar* means "remembering one," and it is used in reference to God's people, which is ironic given their chronic forgetfulness. Psalm 78 lists how the Lord repeatedly provided for the Israelites as he led them from Egypt into the desert, yet they still forgot the Lord and were unfaithful to him. The psalmist said, "Again and again they put God to the test; they vexed the Holy One of Israel. They did not remember his power" (verses 41-42). The psalm goes on to list for a second time all God's incredible works of provision that the Israelites couldn't seem to remember.

The book of Joshua also emphasizes the importance of remembering. The Israelites were standing on the brink of the Promised Land for the second time, and God essentially said, "Okay, let's try this again. I'm giving you the land. Remember that I will be with you, so be strong and courageous. Obey my law. Don't forget to be strong and courageous. And, just in case you didn't hear me, I will be with you." The last time the Israelites were this close to the Promised Land, they balked at the stories of the powerful inhabitants of the land. This time, however, something stuck, and they obeyed. This was a banner day, for the new generation accomplished what the previous generation failed to do—they trusted God and obeyed his commands—and, as a result, witnessed a spectacular example of God's provision. The people prepared to cross into the land, the priests carrying the ark stepped into the river, and the water "piled up in a heap a great distance away" (Joshua 3:16).

Joshua 3:16-17 offers the *Reader's Digest* version of the rest of the story: "So the people crossed over opposite Jericho. The priests who carried the ark of the covenant of the LORD stood firm on dry ground in the middle of the Jordan, while all Israel passed by until the whole nation had completed the crossing on dry ground." Then Joshua 4 gives the expanded version, which emphasizes some memory aids for a forgetful people.

One of these aids is that the people personally witnessed the event. Joshua reported, "As soon as all of them had crossed, the ark of the LORD and the priests came to the other side while the people watched" (verse 11). Seeing this miracle gave the Israelites a visual memory to hold on to. But knowing well the amnesiac tendencies of his people, God gave them something more permanent than a memory.

God commanded Joshua, "Choose twelve men from among the people, one from each tribe, and tell them to take up twelve stones from the middle of the Jordan from right where the priests stood and to carry them over with you and put them down at the place where you stay tonight" (verses 2-3). The stones provided an immediate and tangible reminder of what had just happened. That night the people would have looked at those twelve stones stacked into a pillar (see verse 20) and realized that God had done something awesome. In addition, Joshua explained that the stones would prompt future generations to ask questions ("Daddy, why are those stones piled up like that?"), and this would lead to a retelling of the story.

Our stories are wet, slippery stones snatched from the middle of life's riverbed just before the floodwater comes raging downstream. The stones may have sharp edges that tear into our arms, they may be so heavy that we question whether we can carry them, or they may seem ill-suited for building (God's going to use the abuse in my childhood? He's going to use the cancer that is ravaging my body? He's going to use my child's drug addiction?). But he has a use for these that we can't yet see. We are to take them to Gilgal as Joshua did and there build an altar to God out of the pain and happiness, the suffering and redemption. God has use for the jagged stones as well as the smooth. Our job is to gather them from the riverbed. We invite you to stop, pick up the stones, and tell their stories.

8. Refer back to chapter 3 in *To Be Told.* To your well of stories, add scenes where you saw redemption and where it was absent; where great suffering occurred and where nondramatic, routine suffering occurred; where there was peace and where there was resolution. In other words, add stories of shalom, shalom shattered, shalom sought, and denouement.

9. Quickly sort your stories into categories. You might do this by marking beside each entry an abbreviation for the category it falls into (shalom, shalom shattered, shalom sought, and denouement). Then look back over the list. Which category has the most stories and which has the fewest? Why do you think this is?

10. Look over your list of family stories in chapter 3 of this workbook. What are some recurring themes? Write one of the stories.

11. Which stories are you avoiding? Write a few sentences about one of them.

12. Referring back to your answers to item 5 earlier in this chapter, choose a story where "nothing happened" and write down the facts.

13. Now rewrite the story telling the emotional truth.

For Discussion in Your Story Group—Meeting 4

One of the goals of telling stories in a group is to give and receive constructive feedback and to hear your story as others hear it. As you listen to other group members read their stories, pay attention to your internal reactions. What are you feeling? Are you entertained, interested, bored, burdened, skeptical, angry? Then ask yourself why you feel this way. For example, if you feel irritated, ask yourself if you are feeling sick and therefore *everything* irritates you, or if the story's happy spin on tragic events patronized you. Look for the positive attributes of the story, but don't avoid the negative. The categories below might be helpful as you offer feedback.

"It's a poor sort of memory that only works backwards," the Queen remarked.

—Lewis Carroll, *Through the Looking-Glass and What Alice Found There*

IF THE STORY IS...	ASK YOURSELF...
boring	What details would you like to know? What is the narrator feeling? What is the subtext?
well written	What is being hidden behind the fluidity of the words? What emotions or actions are being downplayed?
sparse	What details would allow you to enter the setting and see the characters? What happened right before this story and/or right after it?
angry	What does the narrator fear? What pain is the narrator feeling or avoiding?
depressing	What does the story reveal about the richness of human interaction? Where, if at all, do you see a small place of hope?
superficial/frivolous	What does this story reveal about interpersonal dynamics? What is being left out?
epic	What does this story avoid with its wide-angle view? What might be revealed if you looked at one scene through a telephoto lens?
painful, but detached	Can you see the narrator in the scene? Does the narrator allow you to feel what she or he is feeling? In what ways?
funny	Where is the pain? Often humor precedes pain. What role does humor play in the narrator's family?
confusing/muddy	What is the narrator avoiding? What really happened? Where is the narrator? If you sketched the scene, would you know where to draw in the narrator?
one where nothing happens	What may be happening in the scene but is left unsaid? What is the emotional plot? What was the author's reason for telling this story? Look for any signs of strong emotion or ambivalence.

1. In your story group, answer question 1 at the beginning of this chapter. Look at the two versions of the truth as the narrator presents them in the passage from *The Things They Carried.* What are the differences between these two truths? In your opinion, is "story-truth" a valid truth? If not, how could you make up for the insufficiencies of "happening-truth"?

2. Have each person read aloud the two versions of their stories when "nothing happened." What deeper truth does each story hold?

Your Well of Stories

As you worked through the chapter, the questions may have reminded you of other scenes. Add these to your well of stories to write later.

stories of shalom

I can remember, at the age of four, holding my pencil in the firm fist grip of a child and transferring the world around me to pieces of paper, margins of books, bare expanses of wall. I remember drawing the contours of that world: my narrow room, with the bed, the paint-it-yourself bureau and desk and chair, the window overlooking the cemented back yard; our apartment, with its white walls and rug-covered floors and the large framed picture of the Rebbe near the living-room window; the wide street that was Brooklyn Parkway, eight lanes of traffic, the red brick and white stone of the apartment houses, the neat cement squares of the sidewalks, the occasional potholes in the asphalt; the people of the street, bearded men, old women gossiping on the benches beneath the trees, little boys in skullcaps and sidecurls, young wives in long-sleeved dresses and fancy wigs—all the married women in our group concealed their natural hair beneath wigs for reasons of modesty. I grew up encrusted with lead and spectrumed with crayons.

—CHAIM POTOK, *My Name Is Asher Lev*

"Paint-it-yourself bureau." "Cemented back yard." "Large framed picture of the Rebbe." "Brooklyn Parkway, eight lanes of traffic." "Little boys in skullcaps and sidecurls." In *My Name Is Asher Lev,* Chaim Potok invites us to step into the world of Hasidic Jews in the

1940s through his descriptions of Crown Heights. We may never have been to Crown Heights, but it comes alive through Potok's descriptions. We walk past the old women on park benches beneath the trees and the young wives with their fancy wigs. Potok's words transport us to the sidewalk of his story.

PAINT THE SETTING

As we write, we use words like an artist uses paint. Through words we transfer the world around us to pieces of paper. With words we capture the sights, smells, textures, sounds, and tastes of a particular time and place. And time and place play a significant role in a story. The setting sets the stage for the characters. A boy with a gift for art, such as Asher Lev, born into a Hasidic community in Brooklyn will have very different experiences from a boy born into a Bohemian community on Paris's Left Bank or a boy born into an Aboriginal community in Australia's outback. The settings impact how each boy expresses his artistic gift as well as how others respond to his gift.

As you think about the settings of your stories, consider these components:

Time. This refers both to time of day and to the era. What was going on politically, socially, and economically during the time of the scene you are describing? What television shows did you watch? What did you do for fun after school?

Place. Where does the story take place? What country, region, state, and area of town? What type of home did you live in, and what was its setting (urban, suburban, small town, rural area with acreage)?

Culture. What beliefs, characteristics, and actions were valued in your social setting? What was the predominant religion? What attitudes did people hold regarding work and leisure? What value did the culture place on education? creativity? athletic ability? physical attractiveness? How did the culture define success? beauty? maturity? love?

Atmosphere. What was the mood and feeling where your story takes place? Was it prosperous? down-and-out? stiff and formal? relaxed and accepting? restrictive? hedonistic?

A story set in summer in the suburbs amid the clattering thrum of lawn mowers and kids playing a pickup baseball game will have a very different feel than one set in government-subsidized urban housing amid the pounding bass of boom boxes and the hand signals of a drug dealer standing on the corner.

1. If you were the set designer for a movie about your life, what details of the setting would be most important for you to include? How would you let your audience know the decade, socioeconomic status, culture, and location of your story? What kind of cars would be on the road? What colors of paint would you choose?

You can jog your memory by referring to books such as *Astonishing Century* by Robert D. Joyce and the *Our American Century* series published by the editors of Time-Life Books. These books contain events, names, titles, and information about popular culture for each year of the twentieth century. High-school yearbooks also frequently include a recap of world events and culture.

The setting of your story impacts the plot, so recalling the setting will help you interpret the action. The same behavior enacted in different settings can have very different meanings. A man with big hair, a brown polyester leisure suit, white loafers, and gold chains around his neck jumps up and dances the Hustle. If this happens at a seventies party, it means one thing. If he strikes his John Travolta pose in the middle of a wedding ceremony, it means another. Is he being funny and celebratory or disruptive and inconsiderate?

Our setting also impacts how we think and what we do. A rule-bound and insincere culture will produce people who are either automatons or rebels. The first stays on the sidewalk even though it's crowded; the second ignores the sign and tromps on the flower beds. Both respond to the environment, but in different ways. Transport the rebel to a biker rally, and suddenly annihilating a couple of daffodils looks tame.

As you write your stories, you may find that the setting has symbolic or ironic

> I prefer winter and fall, when you feel the bone structure in the landscape— the loneliness of it—the dead feeling of winter. Something waits beneath it—the whole story doesn't show.
>
> —ANDREW WYETH, quoted in *The Art of Andrew Wyeth*

meaning as well. A perfectly clean, orderly house may contain people whose highest values are for their children to be happy, successful, and well behaved. The perfection of this house reveals a silent demand for order. Or the setting may contradict the ethos of the story. A bright, orderly house sometimes shelters many dark secrets.

> At bottom, every man knows perfectly well that he is a unique being, only once on this earth; and by no extraordinary chance will such a marvelously picturesque piece of diversity in unity as he is, ever be put together a second time.
> —FRIEDRICH NIETZSCHE

At times the setting has so much power over the characters and the story that it qualifies as a character itself. Some have argued that the Mississippi River is a character in *Huckleberry Finn.* And in William Faulkner's books, the rural Southern county of Yoknapatawpha deeply impacts the lives of its residents.

In the following passages, note how the authors evoke a sense of place.

From the carnival of the street—pushcarts, accordion and fiddle, shoeshine, begging, the dust going round like a woman on stilts—they entered the narrow crowded theater of the brokerage office.[1]
    —Saul Bellow, *Seize the Day*

It was an evening in summer upon the placid and temperate planet Mars. Up and down green wine canals, boats as delicate as bronze flowers drifted. In the long and endless dwellings that curved like tranquil snakes across the hills, lovers lay idly whispering in cool night beds. The last children ran in torchlit alleys, gold spiders in their hands throwing out films of web.[2]
    —Ray Bradbury, *The Martian Chronicles*

We were sitting in the living room of his Victorian house. It was a mansion, really, with fifteen-foot ceilings and large, well-proportioned rooms. A graceful spiral stairway rose from the center hall toward a domed skylight. There was a ballroom on the second floor. It was Mercer House, one of the last of Savannah's great houses still in private hands.[3]
    —John Berendt, *Midnight in the Garden of Good and Evil*

There is a lovely road that runs from Ixopo into the hills. These hills are grass-covered and rolling, and they are lovely beyond any singing of it. The road climbs seven miles into them, to Carisbrooke; and from there, if there is no mist, you look down on one of the fairest valleys of Africa. About you there is grass and bracken and you may hear the forlorn crying of the titihoya, one of the birds of the veld....

The grass is rich and matted, you cannot see the soil. It holds the rain and the mist, and they seep into the ground, feeding the streams in every kloof. It is well-tended, and not too many cattle feed upon it; not too many fires burn it, laying bare the soil. Stand unshod upon it, for the ground is holy, being even as it came from the Creator.[4]

—Alan Paton, *Cry, the Beloved Country*

Maycomb was an old town, but it was a tired old town when I first knew it. In rainy weather the streets turned to red slop; grass grew on the sidewalks, the courthouse sagged in the square. Somehow, it was hotter then: a black dog suffered on a summer's day; bony mules hitched to Hoover carts flicked flies in the sweltering shade of the live oaks on the square. Men's stiff collars wilted by nine in the morning. Ladies bathed before noon, after their three-o'clock naps, and by nightfall were like soft teacakes with frostings of sweat and sweet talcum.[5]

—Harper Lee, *To Kill a Mockingbird*

2. Which phrases in the previous descriptions do you find especially evocative? How might these settings affect the people living in them? the way they view life? their jobs and pastimes? the way they move? what they wear? what they value?

As you play with describing a setting, imagine painting a picture. What colors do you choose? What is clearly visible and what is sketchy? Pay attention to senses other than sight. Close your eyes and slowly "turn on" your other senses. Tune your ears to hear. Awaken the nerve endings in your fingers. Give your taste buds a jiggle. Breathe deeply. What sounds and smells are distinctive to the setting? What texture and taste are important? Give enough detail so that when you write about walking into a room, the readers walk into *your* room and not one they have in *their* minds. Don't worry about being wordy. You can delete unnecessary detail later. Dig into your memory and throw a shovelful of descriptors onto the ground. Then sift through the pile for the jewels you want to keep. Throw out another shovelful, sift through it, and add more jewels to your stash.

> We are a species that needs and wants to understand who we are. Sheep lice do not seem to share this longing, which is one reason they write so very little. But we do. We have so much we want to say and figure out.
>
> —Anne Lamott, *Bird by Bird*

Sometimes holding something physical helps you recreate a past physical setting. As you attempt to paint your stories' settings, find a memento from that time period—a toy, an item of sports equipment, a book—and use it to help you remember. Where did you play with the toy? Describe the room. What color was the flooring? the walls? Was the furniture comfortable? frilly? Photos can also aid your memory, calling to mind the avocado green of your appliances or just how many lace doilies graced your grandmother's furniture. As you look back through photographs, glean details of setting to include in your stories.

*3. In chapter 2 of this workbook, you listed the major settings of your life and described a few of them. Add to the list by dipping into your well of stories and describing the settings. Address the time, place, culture, and atmosphere of several. What is the architecture? How have natural and human forces shaped the topography? What does the furniture look like? You can write phrases that come to mind or a couple of paragraphs.

4. Write about a place from your childhood that elicits strong emotion. Convey a sense of the emotion, but don't name the emotion.

5. Describe a landscape from your life in a way that helps explain the behavior of the people who live there. Describe your home in a way that explains something of who your family was at a specific time.

6. Draw a "memory map"—a map of your neighborhood, your house, your body, or your interior life. Sketch out the physical details of the location you choose, then describe it with words. Think about how the map might be different if you drew it from your perspective as a child.

An infinite number of details inhabit every setting. The trick is picking the details that best portray the place. To practice, choose a couple of your descriptions of setting and see if you can cut them down by half or a quarter of the length without sacrificing their ability to capture the location. This task will require you to search out the "suitcase words"—those words that pack in multiple images.

Reading Passion

In Chaim Potok's book, the artistically gifted Asher Lev is born into a religiously conservative family and culture that view art as both foolish and selfish. His passion for art creates tremendous turbulence in his life as his parents and community struggle with his paintings. Asher's life would have been significantly easier if he had simply put away the Eberhard pencil. His passion led him into conflict and suffering, yet he persisted because he believed his art was good.

Expressing our passions can create both good and evil. A passion for gourmet food can lead to offering hospitality and fine meals to others or to a pattern of gluttony and indulgence. Our passions can lead to comforting those who suffer, creating beauty, and building community, or to a life focused on our own satisfaction.

Read chapter 4, "Listening to What Moves You," in *To Be Told.*

7. What are the yeses that totally changed the direction of your life? When, if ever, have you followed your heart? What happened as a result?

8. What do you most enjoy doing? In what do you find the greatest pleasure and joy? What is it about this idea/person/activity that gives you a sense of life?

9. Consider this statement from *To Be Told:* "We will not know our true self unless we can name the passions that are tied to our ideal self."[6] Describe your ideal self in the areas of worker, friend, spouse, parent, child, citizen, and believer.

10. In chapter 4 of *To Be Told,* we read: "We always choose what we value most, even when the choice does us harm."[7] What do your choices reveal about your passions?

11. What do your passions reveal about what you truly believe about life? yourself? God?

We tend to think of passion in terms of joy. We can be passionate about words or sailing or dancing. But we too easily forget the cost of passion, the suffering that precedes and infuses the joy. Writing, sailing, and dancing all require time and persistence if we are to learn the skills that enable us to do them well. Passion requires sacrifice. The movie *The Passion of the Christ* gives an agonizing picture of suffering fueled by love. Can the slow grind of moving forward through pain be passion? It was for Jesus as he stumbled toward Golgotha. God, who created the wild extravagance of this earth and the intricate complexity of our hearts and minds, created humans to be passionate beings. Passion comes at a high price, but consider the alternative: when we kill our passion, we kill off a part of ourselves as well.

William Butler Yeats wrote the poem "Easter 1916" about the Easter Rising in Ireland. In this clash with the British, many civilians were killed. Yeats's poem talks about the leaders, average people with whom he would exchange nods of the head and "polite, meaningless words" as they walked home from work. But on that Easter

> When you write, you have to attempt something greater than you can possibly hope to accomplish. That is the only way you can leave a hole, a gap—some chance for a miracle.
>
> —HEATHER HARPHAM,
> *I Went to the Animal Fair*

Sunday in 1916, "All changed, changed utterly: / A terrible beauty is born."[8] Walking the path of passion requires the birthing of "a terrible beauty." It costs far more than we would have agreed to if we had known the cost in advance, and yet we would not choose to go back to where we were. Following our hearts changes us utterly, yet it leads to a terrible beauty.

Asher Lev's people, the Hasidic Jews, are known for both how deeply they have suffered and how passionately they celebrate. Their capacity to celebrate is born out of their sorrow—the deeper the well of sorrow is, the deeper the well of joy will be. Those who have not suffered so intensely cannot celebrate so deeply.

Passion often rises out of places of suffering. Someone who has lost a child to cancer is more likely, and more qualified, to begin a support group for parents with dying children than someone who has healthy children. Our passion is meant to be expressed in and for community. We are called to take that which sets our hearts aflame and use it for the benefit of others. In our passions, we catch a glimpse of how God is redeeming the stories of our lives.

*12. What passions have been or might be birthed from your suffering?

13. When has your passion led to suffering in your life?

> My story is important not because it is mine, God knows, but because if I tell it anything like right, the chances are you will recognize that in many ways it is also yours.... It is precisely through these stories in all their particularity, as I have long believed and often said, that God makes himself known to each of us most powerfully and personally. If this is true, it means that to lose track of our stories is to be profoundly impoverished not only humanly but also spiritually.
>
> —Frederick Buechner, *Telling Secrets*

STORIES OF SHALOM

Asher Lev describes the happy times when he was very young, before tragedy struck. He would run through snowdrifts with his mother, row boats in Prospect Park, recite the Krias Shema before going to bed. Often our stories of the deep harmony of shalom come from our early years. In these times of protection and nurture, we get a glimpse of Eden.

Paradoxically, writing these stories of shalom can be painful because the times of tranquillity and innocence have been marred by a fallen world. To remember those seasons, to walk back into those scenes of joy, reminds us of how distant they are. For many, joy scares us more than pain because it stirs up the ache in our souls for heaven. Joy evokes hope for the time when God will wipe away all our tears. We long for the joy of heaven, but we must live in a world where there is abuse, sickness, and crime.

Look back over the section "Shalom" in chapter 3 of *To Be Told*.

14. List some scenes of rest, safety, and warmth from your life and add them to your well of stories.

15. How did these moments both calm and stir you? lead you to rest as well as to awe and wonder?

*16. Choose a scene of shalom and write it.

17. Write a story from your well of stories. As you write, pay special attention to capturing the setting.

> Our stories are what we all carry with us on this trip we take, and we owe it to each other to respect our stories and learn from them.
>
> —William Carlos Williams, quoted in *The Call of Stories*

As you do the exercises in this workbook, remember that you don't have to answer all the questions or write all your stories. You will likely have to push yourself to write, but make it gentle pushing. Let curiosity and hope fuel the pushing. If the number of questions is daunting, try first answering the ones marked with an asterisk; then, if you'd like, go back and jot down quick answers for a few more. Think of the asterisked questions as hors d'oeuvres. They may be just enough. Or they may whet your appetite for the main course.

For Discussion in Your Story Group—Meeting 5

As you listen to each other's stories, pay attention to the setting. Can you place the narrator in the scene? Is she present or does she seem to be floating around? Do you feel removed from the scene as if you're peeking in a window? Are there enough details to help you imagine what the setting looks like? Does the writer employ senses beyond sight to describe the setting?

1. Reread the short, descriptive excerpts from novels earlier in this chapter. Then answer these questions as a group: Which phrases do you find especially evocative? How might these settings affect the people living in them? the way they view life? their jobs and pastimes? the way they move? what they wear? what they value?

2. Which are harder for you to write: stories of shalom or stories of tragedy? Why?

3. Have a few group members read their descriptions of a setting. How would the setting likely impact the people who live there? What does the setting tell you about what the people value? What symbolic or ironic meaning do you see in the setting?

4. Have each person read a story of shalom. At what point(s) does it lead you to rest? to awe and wonder? Which phrases that describe the setting do you find the most evocative?

YOUR WELL OF STORIES

As you worked through the chapter, the questions may have reminded you of other scenes. Add these to your well of stories to write later.

stories of shalom shattered

Estha had always been a quiet child, so no one could pinpoint with any degree of accuracy exactly when (the year, if not the month or day) he had stopped talking. Stopped talking altogether, that is. The fact is that there wasn't an "exactly when." It had been a gradual winding down and closing shop. A barely noticeable quietening. As though he had simply run out of conversation and had nothing left to say. Yet Estha's silence was never awkward. Never intrusive. Never noisy. It wasn't an accusing, protesting silence as much as a sort of estivation, a dormancy, the psychological equivalent of what lungfish do to get themselves through the dry season, except that in Estha's case the dry season looked as though it would last forever.

Over time he had acquired the ability to blend into the background of wherever he was—into bookshelves, gardens, curtains, doorways, streets—to appear inanimate, almost invisible to the untrained eye. It usually took strangers awhile to notice him even when they were in the same room with him. It took them even longer to notice that he never spoke. Some never noticed at all.

Estha occupied very little space in the world.

—ARUNDHATI ROY, *The God of Small Things*

Like a lungfish, Estha shuts down to make it through the dry season. But instead of telling us that Estha is severely depressed, Arundhati Roy offers a picture of how he functions in the world by disappearing. Estha is nearly transparent—he is neither seen nor heard—and yet his silence screams of tragedy and enormous grief in a world that is blind and deaf.

Enflesh the Characters

"Show, don't tell" is one of the mantras of writers. Essentially this guideline means letting readers decipher meaning for themselves instead of telling them what to think. When you show, you draw readers into your story by recreating the experience. In daily life we don't find out that someone is arrogant because she has the word tattooed on her forehead. We experience her arrogance through the look on her face and her word choice, tone of voice, and body language. We use our senses to gather data, and when it adds up to what we define as "arrogant," we summarize it with that one word.

To write with words that show rather than tell, you must play the detective, identifying the clues one by one. Set aside your conclusions for the moment and walk back through the evidence that led to your deduction. Be like Sherlock Holmes who, in story after story, shocks Dr. Watson with his keen observations. In "A Scandal in Bohemia," Holmes picks up on subtle clues and deduces that Watson has resumed his work as a doctor, that he is "into harness" again.

> "In [medical] practice again, I observe. You did not tell me that you intended to go into harness."
>
> "Then, how do you know?"
>
> "I see it, I deduce it. How do I know that you have been getting yourself very wet lately, and that you have a most clumsy and careless servant girl?" [Holmes then explains how he came to his conclusions. He noticed the smell of iodoform and the black mark of silver nitrate on Watson's right forefinger as well as scratches on the edge of his shoe where mud had been scraped off.]

"When I hear you give your reasons," I [Watson] remarked, "the thing always appears to me to be so ridiculously simple that I could easily do it myself, though at each successive instance of your reasoning I am baffled until you explain your process. And yet I believe that my eyes are as good as yours."

"Quite so," he answered.... "You see, but you do not observe."[1]

1. You can tell a great deal about a person by the environment she or he creates. Choose two people from your stories and list what they might carry in their purse, pockets, or car.

Sherlock Holmes's ability to observe made him a brilliant detective. We are detectives in our own lives, piecing together the clues that make up the scenes. Doing this will bring you one step closer to the emotions of the story. You can say simply that someone is arrogant and still be emotionally removed from the scene. But when you write about the arch of her eyebrow, the sneer on her mouth, and the chill in her voice, it places the readers in the scene and enables them to feel its impact.

So as you write your stories, think about how you can show what the person is like without stating it. Instead of saying that the person has compulsive tendencies, show her checking five times to make sure the door is locked. Instead of saying that your father lost his temper, describe the veins bulging in his forehead, the reddening of his face, and his squinty eyes. A physical description of height, weight, and coloring helps the reader visualize the person ("Although he was short and as rotund as a pumpkin…"),

> It's not like Jesus doesn't know all the things you ever done that are wrong without you telling him about them. But until you lay your cards on the table and level with him, they're the great gulf fixed between you. It's only when you tell it to Jesus like it is that they become the Golden Gate Bridge.
>
> —LEO BEBB, in Frederick Buechner, *The Book of Bebb*

but ultimately the person's actions reveal the most about him ("Hubert moved with the speed of a hummingbird, never pausing for longer than a couple of seconds"). Action creates an image that sticks in memory.

As you describe the people in your story, think through how each person is both predictable and unique.

Appearance. Does she wear clothing that is formal? businesslike? sloppy? stylish? hip? Is she well-groomed? How does she stand and move? Is the environment around her chaotic? creative? tidy? comfortably disheveled? austere? elegant? artsy?

Speech. What about his word choice and dialect is distinctive? Is his speech slurred or crisp or in between? How much does he talk and what purpose does the talking serve? Is it relational? purely informational? instructive? attacking? distancing? Does his voice sound gravelly? silky? breathy? squeaky? singsong? Are his words clipped and precise? drawled with dropped consonants? twangy?

> We never know the wine we are becoming while we are being crushed like grapes.
>
> —Henri Nouwen

Actions. What mannerisms does she use? What facial expressions or body language reveal certain emotions? How does she respond to joyful events? tragic events? What role in the family or in relationships does she usually assume? In what ways does she shatter stereotypes? What discrepancies do you notice between the way she acts and what he says?

*2. Look back over your answers to questions about the main characters in your life (questions 1 and 2 in chapter 2) and about family characteristics and speech patterns (questions 2, 3, and 5 in chapter 3). Choose a couple of these people and write a paragraph or two describing each of them.

3. How would you show, instead of merely tell, the emotions below? Describe what you would see and hear in the face, body language, and voice of a person who feels…

   joy

   cold anger

   loneliness

   grief

   rage

   amusement

   contempt

4. What metaphors or similes would you use to describe the emotions listed in question 3? (For example, a person who feels crazy might look like shattered glass. A person who is angry may have daggers shooting from his eyes and a nail gun in his mouth ready to permanently affix someone to the wall.)

Stories of Shalom Shattered

Stories not told and tragedies left unspoken weigh heavily on Estha and his twin, Rahel, in *The God of Small Things.* The twins try to make sense of the drowning of their eight-year-old cousin and the surrounding tragic events. When Estha is sexually abused, that event is simply more debris in a life logjammed with the injustices of India's caste system, abuse, abandonment, and violence. Estha can't articulate his confusion, guilt, and pain, so he doesn't speak at all. For seven-year-olds Estha and Rahel, shalom has been shattered.

Read chapter 5, "Facing the Tragedy That Shapes You," and the section "Shalom Shattered" in chapter 3 of *To Be Told.* What are your tragedies? Some people would say they've had no great tragedies in their lives. Yes, bad things have happened, but overall life has been all right. You may feel that you have nothing to write about. If you have not explored the tragedies in your life, it may be hard to identify them. It is like looking at land on the horizon from the crow's nest of a sailing ship or the bow of an outrigger canoe. You see broad contours, but not much more. As the boat approaches land, you notice that the mountains, streams, trees, and beaches gain definition. You spot a tiger in the underbrush and see an enormous boa constrictor lounging in a tree. But when you're at sea, you see none of this. Write of what you do see, then row closer. Step onto the beach and walk up to that boa constrictor, look into its unblinking eyes, and continue to write.

> It hurts to feel life. To pause. To stop and listen to your own breathing. But you have to lay yourself open to it all. Because that's where God is. There is no life apart from God, because God is not apart from life. If you turn away, if you run, you will miss both.
>
> —Heather Harpham,
> *I Went to the Animal Fair*

Other people have lives so marked by tragedy that there seems to be very little else. For these people, the boat has run aground and lies broken on ragged rocks. Tigers pace where jungle meets beach and salivate in anticipation. Leaving the debris of the ship and wading ashore will require courage you're not sure you can muster.

The only reason to step off the boat and explore the land is if you believe that the place of tragedy offers something life-giving. Stories of tragedy will be painful to write.

Why risk tangling with the tigers unless you are convinced that riches are buried in the poisoned soil? The intrepid explorer believes that what our tragedies reveal about God and ourselves is worth the risk of tiger and snake. We write not for the purpose of catharsis but to expose the areas where we have refused to trust God. We study our stories because we hope that by learning from the past, we can create a richer future.

A friend who is a nurse told the story of a woman who refused pain medication during the delivery of her stillborn child. She caused a stir among the hospital's medical staff. They could understand a woman refusing medicine because she wanted to more fully experience the emergence of life from her womb, but they could not comprehend why this woman would choose to add severe physical pain to her intense emotional suffering. Later she explained that in her culture pain is considered an important part of the grieving process, and she didn't want to numb herself to the agony of losing a baby and thereby numb herself to the rest of life. The contractions of her body reflected the writhing of her heart.

This is not an argument for refusing pain medication but a picture of the cost of embracing pain. In choosing to welcome pain instead of run from it, we will feel the full measure of the anguish. The alternative—escape—offers only temporary reprieve. We can choose numbness, but in doing so we will miss out on whatever the pain has to teach us. Numbness merely masks the truth. We can ignore our stories or learn from them and vastly enrich our lives in the process. Through the pain, new life will be birthed.

5. What do you feel about the idea that pain can potentially refine and bless you and enable you to experience more joy?

*6. What is the difference between resolving your past and using your past for the sake of growth?

7. Is it harder for you to see the great suffering and sorrow or the incandescent beauty of this life? Why?

8. A wise man once said, "Jesus always gives you what he knew you would have asked for if you knew everything he knows." What would you like to say to God in response to this idea?

God uses our tragedies to teach us about himself. How will we know of God's power unless we see him redeem our tragedies? How will we know of his suffering on our behalf unless we enter into our own suffering? In the Old Testament, when God's people experienced his provision and protection, they lapsed into forgetfulness. When we are satisfied, we easily forget our dependence on God. He uses tragedy to call us back to himself. Tragedy compels our attention in a way shalom never could. Only our hope for healing and redemption are sufficient reasons to face the tiger. It's useless to remain in the broken boat. And nothing was ever discovered by those who refused to wade ashore.

All of us are cut down by great tragedies and pummeled by routine suffering. Our tragedies may be as catastrophic as losing several family members in a car crash or as mundane as trying to raise children on minimum wage. But no matter what form they take, tragedies lead us to places where we feel powerless, betrayed, and ambivalent, places where we become the orphan, the stranger, and the widow. Our world tilts off balance, and the best we can do is hold on and hope for a return of stability.

The powerlessness we feel leads to the despair, deadness, loneliness, and hopelessness of an orphan, a child alone in a world that preys on the weak and unprotected. We long to see our Father's face, hear his blessing, and feel the warmth of both his protection of and his delight in us. We long for him to tell us who we are and what we were uniquely made to do. In the absence of this, the weeds of despair and apathy grow. We begin to believe that it doesn't matter what we do because, we've concluded, nothing will change anyway.

> All art, therefore, appeals primarily to the senses, and the artistic aim when expressing itself in written words must also make its appeal through the senses, if its high desire is to reach the secret spring of responsive emotions.... My task which I am trying to achieve is, by the power of the written word to make you hear, to make you feel—it is, before all, to make you see. That—and no more, and it is everything.
>
> —JOSEPH CONRAD,
> *The Nigger of the "Narcissus"*

We long, too, for close friendships. When the tragedy of betrayal strikes, it destroys our trust and shatters our joy. Betrayal can range from blatantly deceiving and using another person to simply refusing to see or act on behalf of someone who is being harmed. Betrayal fuels suspicion, anger, and shame that we were duped. It gives rise to a determination not to be vulnerable and humiliated again. In its wake we become strangers, facing the loneliness of broken friendships and longing for the wholeness that comes from being part of a loving, trustworthy community. Betrayal spawns doubt, kills faith, and induces hypervigilance. And the hypervigilant are exhausted people.

Finally, when we experience the tragic failure of love, ambivalence takes root. When we lose our lover through death, desertion, or the distance of emotional disengagement, of if we have never been chosen by another, we will approach new relationships with conflicting emotions. We want to be loved, but we don't want to be harmed, abandoned, or even called to a new level of strength and tenderness. To allow ourselves to be loved is to risk being hurt by love's failures. Instead we become widows who feel naked and unprotected and who ache for the embrace and tenderness of our lover. Tossed around by our ambivalence, we become either defensive or demanding in order to protect ourselves. We love out of duty, and we refuse to really engage another with integrity and hope. Instead we work to prop up the status quo.[2]

*9. List some instances when you have felt…
    powerless/despairing/apathetic

    betrayed/hypervigilant/exhausted

    ambivalent/defensive or demanding/dutiful

    and when you have been…
    an orphan, fatherless and unprotected

    a stranger, alone and without a friend

    a widow, rejected or not chosen

10. At what points in your life has God seemed absent?

    If you feel emotionally detached as you write about your tragedies, you may find it helpful to hold the pen with your nondominant hand. The strain of figuring out how to form letters with muscles not trained to do so forces you to choose fewer, more expressive words. Jagged lines and poorly formed letters express a gut-level agony that beautiful penmanship and electronic words tend to mask. Also, if your story is about a childhood tragedy, writing in this way can help you get in touch with the feelings of being a child. If you happen to be ambidextrous, try writing with you toes.

> Where there is ruin, there is hope for treasure.
>
> —RUMI, quoted in *Traveling Mercies*

Sometimes in the wake of a tragedy, we vow to protect ourselves against future harm: "I will never love someone so much that he or she could really harm me," "I will never again tell others about my marital problems," "I will not need other people." Then, consciously or unconsciously, we bring the rules we have made for ourselves into our relationships.

11. What vows have you made? Identify and describe the stories behind those vows.

12. How have your tragedies shaped your view of the world and how you function in it? Note both the beneficial and destructive effects.

*13. Add the stories above to your well of stories, then choose one and write about it.

One of the most troublesome of God's characteristics is that he rarely takes away the messes of our lives. God redeems *through* harm, not *from* harm. We discover his fingerprints in the midst of the stories of our lives, not outside them. But when things don't make sense, we either conclude that God doesn't know what he is doing or we try to soothe the ache by rationalizing and diminishing the pain. As you write about tragedy, resist the urge to find a moral in your story. Be aware of when you try to cover anger with trite aphorisms. We sacrifice both our integrity and an opportunity for growth when we avoid suffering with cloying platitudes like "Just trust God," "Time heals all wounds," or "It will all work out in the end." Allow yourself to sit in the grief and pain and to hope for the day when God's presence with you in your tragedy becomes clear. He can withstand both your grief and your anger. Wrestle with him as Jacob did. You will walk away with both a limp and a blessing.

> Life is pain, Highness. Anyone who tells you differently is selling something.
>
> —Dread Pirate Roberts, in the movie *The Princess Bride*

In some ways, tragedy marks the true beginning of our story. It "introduces us to ourselves, to our deepest passions, to what it is that receives either our yes or our no."[3] When we experience tragedy, we see how suffering shapes our characters. God often uses our tragedies to give us compassion for others who suffer in the same way we have suffered.

14.   What have your tragedies revealed to you about God's heart for humanity? Who are the people you feel most called to love and serve, and what are their circumstances?

15.   What passions have you seen arise from the ashes of your tragedies?

In Valiska Gregory's beautiful book *Through the Mickle Woods,* a wise bear tells three stories to a grieving king. In one, an owl visits a weaver who spins stories. The owl tells her he wishes his story to be woven of clouds. She does so, but it falls apart. He then brings other beautiful things, but the story weaving always dissolves. The owl is puzzled, and the weaver tells him, "You must bring everything, things chosen and things not." So the owl gathers everything he can find and takes it to the weaver. "She took the things the owl had brought—threads of sunlight fine as silk and cobwebs gray as skulls—and wove them all together into a cloth. And when the owl pulled his story round him, it was so full of woe and gladness, so beautiful and strong, that when he stretched out his new-made wings, people thought he was an angel hovering in a breathless sky."[4]

God weaves his goodness through both the woe and gladness of our lives, creating a story that is beautifully tender and strong.

16. Name some of the threads of woe and gladness that God has woven into your life.

FOR DISCUSSION IN YOUR STORY GROUP—MEETING 6

As you listen to others' stories of shalom shattered, be aware of what you feel. Do you desire to fix things? Do you want to say something that will help the person trust God and move on? Are you looking for evidence that the story is not as bad as it seems?

Listening to stories of tragedy can be painful, especially if you care very much for the people telling the stories. Wanting to fix the situation or find the silver lining may seem helpful, but such responses are merely fool's gold, readily available at a low cost. God mines gold from our stories that is far more valuable. But it is buried deep, and getting to it requires labor and patience and suffering. Many times the best gift you can offer others is the gift of your presence, compassion, sorrow, and willingness to wait with them for God to reveal the gold.

1. Have a couple of people in your group read their descriptions from question 1 in this chapter: Choose two people from your stories and list what they might carry in their purses, pockets, or cars. Then, using only that description, make some guesses about what that person is like.
2. Answer this chapter's question 6 in the group: What is the difference between resolving your past and using your past for the sake of growth?
3. How have your tragedies shaped your view of the world and how you function in it? Note both the beneficial and destructive effects.
4. Have each person read a personal story of shalom shattered. What would you like to say to God in response to each story? How does the story reveal (show) character through description, dialogue, and actions?

Your Well of Stories

As you worked through the chapter, the questions may have reminded you of other scenes. Add these to your well of stories to write later.

stories of shalom sought

All the house was still; for I believe all, except St. John and myself, were now retired to rest. The one candle was dying out: the room was full of moonlight. My heart beat fast and thick: I heard its throb. Suddenly it stood still to an inexpressible feeling that thrilled it through, and passed at once to my head and extremities. The feeling was not like an electric shock, but it was quite as sharp, as strange, as startling: it acted on my senses as if their utmost activity hitherto had been but torpor, from which they were now summoned and forced to wake. They rose expectant: eye and ear waited while the flesh quivered on my bones.

"What have you heard? What do you see?" asked St. John. I saw nothing, but I heard a voice somewhere cry—

"Jane! Jane! Jane!"—nothing more.

"O God! what is it?" I gasped.

I might have said, "Where is it?" for it did not seem in the room, nor in the house, nor in the garden; it did not come out of the air, nor from under the earth, nor from overhead. I had heard it—where, or whence, for ever impossible to know! And it was the voice of a human being—a known, loved, well-remembered voice—that of Edward Fairfax Rochester; and it spoke in pain and woe, wildly, eerily, urgently.

"I am coming!" I cried. "Wait for me! Oh, I will come!" I flew to the door and looked into the passage: it was dark. I ran out into the garden: it was void.

—Charlotte Brontë, *Jane Eyre*

When God created humans, he created not automatons but rational, creative beings with both memory of the past and awareness that there is a future. In order to have the relationship with us that he wants, God honors us with choice even when that choice involves running away from him. Just prior to this scene from *Jane Eyre*, St. John pressures Jane Eyre to marry him, and she nearly relents. Then she hears the beloved voice cry out her name. What looked like a straight path laid out before her turns a sharp corner. St. John has written the plot of Jane's future for her, but Jane picks up the pen herself and writes. He wants to possess her, but Jane honors her humanity by refusing to be possessed.

God, too, is a Lover who wants to possess us, but his possession does not consume and destroy us. He wants us for himself because there we can be truly free. And in that freedom, he allows us to write the plots of our lives.

Plot Your Plot

A story's plot is not merely a listing of events: this happened and then that happened and then this other thing happened. In *Aspects of the Novel*, E. M. Forster defined story and plot. "'The king died and then the queen died' is a story. 'The king died, and then the queen died of grief' is a plot."[1] A story records events in chronological order and prompts us to ask, "And then what?" A plot arranges events to reveal their significance and leads us to the question "Why?" Plot creates the links between the events. With a story, we hear what happens; with a plot, we understand.

Forster came down a bit hard on stories. If we substitute *tale* for *story*, his distinction may be clearer. In a tale, two-dimensional characters participate in a series of events. Think "Goldilocks and the Three Bears" or a typical action movie. *Plot,* too, can be a troublesome word. A story or book that is plot-driven relies too heavily on relating a sequence of events and is read merely for the excitement of finding out what happens next. A plot-driven book usually sacrifices depth in characters and richness of insight for the sake of a thrill.

In this workbook, we use the word *story* to mean the whole package—plot, characters, setting, themes—so you may find it helpful to think in terms of a poor story versus a good story. A poor story has shallow characters who act in predictable ways and a plot that is simply a sequence of events. In a good story, plot, character, and setting work together to provide richness, depth, and insight. Characters are more complex and therefore more human.

> Grace is a lover undressing the soul.
> —ROBERT DEEBLE, "Eclipse,"
> *Thirteen Stories* CD

When diagrammed, plot looks like a mountain. It begins at a level place of peace but moves quickly up the incline to conflict. At the peak, the action reaches a crisis or climax, which, once resolved, allows the plot to descend to a place of denouement. In life you will have many cycles of this shalom/shalom shattered/shalom sought/denouement pattern in your life, and sometimes the cycles will overlap. God will redeem some tragedies quickly, and you will enjoy a period of denouement. He may choose to take decades or a lifetime to redeem other tragedies. You may simultaneously come to a place of denouement in one area of your life and new shatterings of shalom in another. Plot may be found in one short scene that has rising and falling action or through a dozen scenes that, read together, create an integrated story.

1. Choose one of the stories that you have written and chart the plot. Where do you see shalom, shalom shattered, shalom sought, and denouement? It's possible that the story you choose may not have all four components.

Shalom shattered is a place of tragedy, but it also can be understood in literary terms as a place of conflict. We want power over our world and connection with others, and these two desires propel our stories forward yet lead to great strife. Our desire to have some control or power over our lives can be seen in many categories of conflict: person vs. person, person vs. nature, person vs. machine, person vs. society, person vs. God, person vs. herself/himself. We find ourselves dealing with tornadoes, broken lawnmowers, skirmishes with our coworkers, unjust laws, a God who does not prevent tragedy, and our own consciences. We also desire to belong to a community that cares for us, so we struggle with the connections and disconnections that come in human relationships.[2]

2. Choose several of your stories and list the conflicts and the motivations that led to them. What pattern do you see? Do your actions suggest that you care more about power or connection? Explain.

3. What motivates each of the people in your story? What does each person want most? What stands in the way?

4. Read the section "What Sort of Plot Does Your Story Have?" in chapter 1 of *To Be Told*. Write down some of the family stories that predate you but have had great impact on your life.

5. Write about your parents' courtship. Describe your parents' relationships with their parents and with the rest of their families.

6. Into what kind of situation were you born (for example: rich, poor, loving, abusive)? Where do you fall in the birth order? What differences have these situations made in your life?

SHALOM SOUGHT

"I am coming!" Jane Eyre cries, even though seeking Edward Rochester requires her to walk back into tragedy. Jane is betrothed to Rochester but discovers on her wedding day that he is still married to a violent, insane woman who lives in the attic. Jane chooses to leave because she loves him and respects herself too much to be his mistress. The leaving not only breaks her heart but also plunges her into financial destitution. Paradoxically, through the loss of one family, Jane, an orphan, finds another in St. John and his sisters. In returning to Rochester, Jane seeks shalom, but of a different sort. She does not return in order to be his wife but to care for him, for he is now blind. But the shalom she finds is different, and more glorious, than both that which was shattered and that for which she hoped.

Read the section "Shalom Sought" in chapter 3 of *To Be Told*. The search for shalom requires a hope that things are not as ravaged as they seem or that beauty can be plucked from the midst of the ruins. This search implies the hope that the answer to the question "Is life meaningful?" is yes. Seeking shalom is not a quick fix or a matter of jerry-building meaning where there is none. The search for shalom requires us to grasp shreds of hope in the midst of heartache and suffering. Sometimes that grasping means simply clinging to the belief that God is good even when everything around us testifies against that. To seek shalom, therefore, we must have the courage and integrity to face how shalom has been shattered. Otherwise, in our seeking we will be satisfied when we find fool's gold and will not dig deeper to uncover the real thing.

> Writing is an act of faith.
>
> —E. B. White, *The Elements of Style*

After all, if God truly is good beyond our wildest imagining and if God takes evil and uses it for good, then how God redeems the tragedies of our lives will be nothing short of glorious. We may not see the redemption in this lifetime. But then again, God just may do the redeeming right now.

Our tragedy is also our redemption. God allows tragedy because he can use it to soften our hearts and make them more his own. Like Rochester, we can't love in a way that is truly selfless until we are broken. Often God uses our tragedies to give us compassion for others who suffer in the same way. God takes what was meant for evil and uses it for good. We are called to do the same.

7. What is your response to this statement from *To Be Told:* "Life is not predictable. The simple equation, 'Do good and good will come to you, but do bad and you will pay the price,' doesn't hold. It is more accurate to say, 'Do good or do bad, but in either case disaster awaits.' "[3]

*8. What would you like to offer those who suffer in the same ways you have suffered?

9. Consider this statement: "We live story vicariously through television, sports, magazines, and talk shows. Such stories may occasionally educate us, but most often they sedate us. They free us from admitting that our own life is dull and lifeless. They attract us because they offer life without risk. They are deadly safe."[4] How do you attempt to escape the risk and tragedy of life?

10. Though fantasy may arise from legitimate desire, it is bloodless. Fantasy is a dream without suffering. About what do you fantasize? About what do you dream?

OUR BELOVED ENEMY

In the book of Hosea, God instructs his prophet to marry an adulterous woman in order to be a living mirror of God's relationship with the Israelites. So Hosea marries Gomer, and they have three children. But marital bliss is short-lived as Gomer runs after lovers who give her gifts of linen, oil, and drink. The second chapter of Hosea contains the outraged cry of a betrayed spouse. He will take away the gifts he gave, expose her unfaithfulness, stop her celebrations, ruin her vines, and punish her (see verses 9-13). Midway through the chapter, however, his tone changes: "Therefore I am now going to allure her; I will lead her into the desert and speak tenderly to her" (verse 14). He does not want to destroy her. He simply wants her back.

The Hebrew word *pathah* means "to open, make roomy" or "to delude: allure, deceive, entice, flatter."[5] The word appears twenty-five times in the Bible, and in all but two of those instances, *pathah* means to convince someone to walk unknowingly, but of his or her own accord, into destruction. In many cases there is evil intent and deception. Sometimes the word has sexual connotations, sometimes it describes a maneuver in war, and other times it refers to being led away from God, as in "Be careful, or you will be enticed *[pathah]* to turn away and worship other gods" (Deuteronomy 11:16).

> And here in dust and dirt, O here,
> The lilies of his love appear.
>
> —GEORGE HERBERT, "The Revival"

So it is telling that in Hosea the word *pathah* describes how God will interact with his adulterous people. God does not use force, but the methods he uses are nearly irresistible. In Hosea, the word *pathah* is translated "allure." God declares that he will *pathah*—delude, allure, deceive, entice, flatter—Israel. God, the cuckolded husband, will seduce his wife away from her lovers. She must choose, but he will provide plenty of incentive. He will decimate her in order to restore her to himself. But it will be her choice to return.

God wants Israel to be completely his, but in order to reach her, he must show her how desolate life is without him. So he leads her into the desert, a barren place where she must face her neediness, and speaks tenderly to her. He wants her, but on his terms, not hers. In the same way, God uses the wasteland of our tragedies to draw us to him. He allows our hard hearts to be broken so he can make them more alive and tender. In *The Magnificent Defeat,* Frederick Buechner calls God our "beloved enemy."

> Power, success, happiness, as the world knows them, are his who will fight for them hard enough; but peace, love, joy, are only from God. And God is the enemy whom Jacob fought there by the river, of course, and whom in one way or another we all of us fight—God, the beloved enemy. Our enemy because, before giving us everything, he demands of us everything; before giving us life, he demands our lives—our selves, our wills, our treasure.
>
> Will we give them, you and I? I do not know. Only remember the last glimpse that we have of Jacob, limping home against the great conflagration of the dawn. Remember Jesus of Nazareth, staggering on broken feet out of the tomb toward the Resurrection, bearing on his body the proud insignia of

the defeat which is victory, the magnificent defeat of the human soul at the hands of God.[6]

The story of Hosea and Gomer, God and Israel, offers a glorious picture of shalom sought and the redemption of tragedy. God/Hosea not only pursues the betrayer, but also offers her something far more precious than the relationship they had prior to her betrayal. God/Hosea says that Israel/Gomer will call him "my husband" instead of "my master" (Hosea 2:16), indicating a much more intimate relationship, one based on love rather than duty. He tells her:

> I will betroth you to me forever;
>> I will betroth you in righteousness and justice,
>> in love and compassion.
> I will betroth you in faithfulness,
>> and you will acknowledge the LORD. (verses 19-20)

The Lord of the universe longs to bathe us with love and compassion, and he invites us into the passion of a marriage relationship with him.

11. How has God used tragedy in your life to draw you to himself? How has God allured, enticed, seduced you? How has he defeated you in order to win you to himself?

WHAT WE SEEK

In her book *My First White Friend,* Patricia Raybon tells a story of racial violence from her childhood.

A "bad" girl chased me home from school one day, pelting me upside the head finally with one solid snowball fortified with a rock. Mama walked me to the girl's house—to settle the score. That's what I thought. But when the tough girl came out on to her porch, Mama looked her over, then gently pulled the child into her arms and simply asked a question: "What's wrong, baby? Why did you do this?"

This hard girl, tough as nails, heard Mama's steady, soft voice, that Southern softness—felt the warm arms holding her close, granting her love and simple forgiveness—and the girl instantly started crying, tears running like rushing water. She was melting into the acceptance of the human touch, not caring that I—who'd fled her threats only an hour before—was watching, gape-eyed, while she blubbered now like a baby. Then Mama, pointing to me, firmly told the girl that "Patricia isn't your enemy"—in fact, I would be her friend. *I would?* Mama looked at me solidly and her eyes firmly answered.[7]

Patricia Raybon's mother sought shalom on Patricia's behalf. She did not want her daughter to have to endure either an uneasy truce or a covert war. She sought a relationship based on forgiveness and mutual respect. And she did so by entering the tough girl's story and defeating her with love, much as God/Hosea did for Israel/Gomer.

Tragedy shatters shalom and leaves in its wake a desert of powerlessness, betrayal, and ambivalence. Whether the tragedy is of our own making or perpetrated on us by others, God uses that hostile place to woo us into a more intimate relationship with him. Thus, faith, hope, and love grow in tragedy's desiccated landscape. God leads his people to the desert and says, "There I will give her back her vineyards, and will make the Valley of Achor ["trouble"] a door of hope. There she will sing as in the days of her youth, as in the day she came up out of Egypt" (Hosea 2:15).

Of course we struggle with the doubt and mistrust that spring from betrayal. We find ourselves strangers, alone and friendless. But we are called to trust that the God who leads us to the desert intends it for our good. Faith requires not an absence of doubts, but a willingness to walk toward God despite them, to say, "I do believe; help me overcome my unbelief!" (Mark 9:24). There is more faith in the angry question, "God, why did you let this happen?" than in the pleasant platitude, "I'm just trusting God." The first implies relationship with God; the second shuts out both God and the pain. Faith involves telling our stories and searching for God's fingerprints on them. We are betrayed strangers, but God calls us to trust him.

As orphans, we encounter the despair of powerlessness, yet we are called to hope for the future. Hope is not mere optimism. True hope requires the ballast of suffering and honesty. True hope stares down pain and fear and waits expectantly for God to appear. And hope gives us the freedom to play with the plots of our lives, to rewrite our future. God invites powerless orphans to hope and rest in the fact that he is our Father who writes our stories with us.

> The best way to predict the future is to invent it.
>
> —ALAN KAY, chief scientist, Apple Computer

As widows, we protect ourselves by loving out of duty—by not allowing ourselves to trust or be vulnerable—but God woos us to a place where we will love with passion. Love is more than simply being nice. The Pharisees, the rich young ruler, and many others would not call Jesus's love nice. Jesus loved them so much that he was willing to confront them. We will love with more passion as we experience God's passionate, extravagant love for ambivalent widows.

God takes the Valley of Achor, a place of great vulnerability, and creates a way of escape. He makes a valley into a door and transforms trouble into hope. He takes betrayal, powerlessness, and ambivalence and creates faith, hope, and love. He takes strangers, orphans, and widows and makes us friends, children, and lovers.

12. What stories of your life have led you to deeper places of faith, hope, and love?

*13. Choose one of the stories from question 12, or another story of shalom sought and the journey to redeem tragedy, and write it.

CATCHING OUR CALLING

Creation reveals an extravagant God. He tossed stars into the sky, invented bizarre insects, and made humans so that we are wildly different from one another and yet very much the same. God is extravagant, yet he doesn't waste anything. Tragedies, moments of glory, and the mundane are all currency in God's economy. God uses all of these for his purposes. He also discloses our callings through the patterns of the past.

Read chapter 6, "Getting Caught by Your Calling," in *To Be Told*.

14. What observations and passing comments have other people—friends, coworkers, neighbors, acquaintances, enemies, employers, clients—made about your abilities? character strengths and weaknesses? giftedness?

*15. Talk to people who know, love, and respect you. Ask them how they experience you when you are hurt, angry, afraid, lonely, confident, jubilant, and at rest. Encourage them to offer (gently) negative as well as positive comments.

It likely will be difficult to ask for this feedback and to hear it without getting defensive or dismissing it. Your first reaction to hearing negative feedback may be to think, "But you're worse than me because you *x!*" (Fill in *x* with whatever horrible thing the other person does.) When you want to defend yourself, take a deep breath instead. Let these people offer you the gift of a mirror. Invite them to speak their words with kindness, humility, and mercy, but even if they don't, you can still learn from them. As you listen to what these people say, collect all the information, even if you believe their input to be misguided or worthless. You can sort through it later.

Positive feedback may also make you uncomfortable. If you are tempted either to dismiss what the other person says as no big deal or to counter with how you have failed in that area, resist that urge and keep gathering information. Yes, you are a flawed being, but God created in you great beauty as well. To deny that beauty is to deny God's goodness.

16. What patterns, overlapping concepts, and repeated ideas do you find in feedback about how people experience you? Where did these patterns come from? What stories lie behind them?

17. Write one of the stories that led to a pattern in your life.

18. Is it more difficult for you to hear a critique or a compliment? Why? What stories lie behind your answer?

Greg and Sophia worship a crazy God. February 8, 1997, was the day Greg decided to be honest with Sophia about his struggles with sexual addiction. Late the night before, he had flown home to Boston from a two-month work project in San Francisco. It had turned into a two-month sexual binge, worse than anything he had done before, and his life was a mess.

That morning Greg decided that he could not keep lying to Sophia. What followed was the darkest day of his life as he watched her physically crumple under the weight of his words. After she left their apartment, Greg decided that he had two options: God would have to work a miracle or Greg would kill himself. A miracle felt impossible, so Greg began planning his death. As he was writing the suicide note, Sophia returned. She had been gone for only fifteen minutes.

"I haven't done what you've done, but I've hurt you, and sin is sin," she told him. "I'm guilty too." Greg was angry. He had shredded Sophia's heart, yet she had come back. And her words were not what he wanted to hear. She had *not* done what he had done. He told her to leave, but she refused.

That was the beginning of a long journey of pain and healing. Greg met with his pastor, who asked him if he would be willing to talk with another man in the church who faced similar struggles. The pastor made a phone call, and a few minutes later Greg was stunned when a man whom he highly respected and loved walked into the office. They met weekly for two years. Feeling that he had nothing to lose, Greg was open about his addiction, and people came out of the woodwork to tell him about their own struggles. Greg and Sophia's lives fell apart, but God put in place a community to help them pick up the pieces.

> One man is not better than another because he is a lawyer while the other is a painter. A life is measured by how it is lived for the sake of heaven.
>
> —Chaim Potok, *My Name Is Asher Lev*

Several years later Greg left a career in software development to attend graduate school in counseling and theology, and he felt drawn to sex-addiction therapy. He signed up for a seminar in Arizona as part of certification as a sex-addiction therapist. On the plane he realized that it was February 8, 2003. That day, exactly six years before, he had told Sophia the truth. In 1997, February 8 was a day of suicidal darkness. In

2003, February 8 was a day of great hope. What had nearly killed Greg has been redeemed through his work of counseling and leading recovery groups for people who struggle with sexual addiction. It is now a wildly blessed time in Greg's life. He went from disliking people to loving being with people. He asked for a miracle and received it, but the path and the destination were far crazier than he could have imagined.

Sophia suggested that while Greg was at the seminar he find something to mark the time and how God was working. Greg walked into old Scottsdale to look for a piece of art, but hours of searching turned up nothing. On the way back to Boston, he stopped in a kitschy airport store, and there he saw God.

Actually, what Greg saw was a furry, stuffed, multicolored Kokopelli, the hump-backed, flute-playing prankster, healer, and storyteller that is a sacred figure to Native Americans in the Southwest. For Greg, his Kokopelli represents the crazy playfulness and unexpected redemptive work of God. Greg's Kokopelli is beady eyed and long legged with weird yellow things coming out of his head and a crazy grin that says, in Greg's words, "I got ya and I ain't lettin' go." It's a reminder that God does not look or act as we expect him to and that he is both serious and whacked.

Your calling may not involve a career change and graduate school. It may mean starting a recovery group in your church. Or it may mean doing something crazier than you can imagine.

19. What inklings do you have of God's calling for you?

For Discussion in Your Story Group—Meeting 7

Your story group has met for six weeks, and you've heard at least six stories from each person. Take a few minutes to talk about how the group is going. Does everyone have the opportunity to participate? Do you feel that you are able to hear the stories well—

with understanding and compassion? Remember to be aware of how you listen and respond to the stories of others. If you find yourself thinking of what you are going to say next or wanting to counter with a story of your own, pause for a moment so you can really listen to what the other person is saying. Many of the stories that people bring to the group have never been told before this. Honor the storyteller by listening well and giving the story space.

1. Think of a movie that everyone in the group has seen and plot the plot. What were the main conflicts? What motivated the characters?

2. Have each person in the group answer question 15 to help you gather information about your calling. Ask the group members how they experience you when you are hurt, angry, afraid, lonely, confident, jubilant, and at rest. Encourage them to offer negative as well as positive comments. Be honest, but also remember to be gracious and kind with your feedback to others.

3. Have group members give a short synopsis of the stories they've told so far. Think through each collection of stories. What patterns do you see?

4. Have each person read a story of shalom sought. What glimpses of God's calling for the reader do you see in the story? Trace the rise and fall of the plot in the story.

Your Well of Stories

As you worked through the chapter, the questions may have reminded you of other scenes. Add these to your well of stories to write later.

chapter eight

story stones and theme altars

[Norman and his father wait as his brother Paul finishes catching his limit of trout.]

I [Norman] scrambled up the bank and asked him, "How many did you get?" He [Norman's father] said, "I got all I want." I said, "But how many did you get?" He said, "I got four or five." I asked, "Are they any good?" He said, "They are beautiful."

He was about the only man I ever knew who used the word "beautiful" as a natural form of speech, and I guess I picked up the habit from hanging around him when I was little.

"How many did you catch?" he asked. "I also caught all I want," I told him. He omitted asking me just how many that was, but he did ask me, "Are they any good?" "They are beautiful," I told him, and sat down beside him.

"What have you been reading?" I asked. "A book," he said. It was on the ground on the other side of him. So I would not have to bother to look over his knees to see it, he said, "A good book."

Then he told me, "In the part I was reading it says the Word was in the beginning, and that's right. I used to think water was first, but if you listen carefully you will hear that the words are underneath the water."

"That's because you are a preacher first and then a fisherman," I told him. "If you ask Paul, he will tell you that the words are formed out of water."

"No," my father said, "you are not listening carefully. The water runs over the words. Paul will tell you the same thing."

—NORMAN MACLEAN, *A River Runs Through It*

The image of a river runs through Norman Maclean's evocative, poetic novella of life and love and the art of fly-fishing. The river represents grace; it's a place of worship and beauty; and it has similarities with stories. Maclean writes, "Stories of life are often more like rivers than books."[1] Some stories flow deep, smooth, and wide. Some frolic and crash through fields of boulders, creating class-five rapids. Others circle back on themselves, forming quiet eddies, then rush and tumble over a cliff and crash on the rocks below, and later become subdued and flow tranquilly through the roots of overhanging trees. Fishermen learn to "read the water" to discern where the big trout might be hiding or where the river runs shallow enough that they can wade across. In the same way, we read our lives in order to recognize the patterns. Just as the fisherman reads the water, we study the contours of our lives, the pools and rapids, the trickles and raging floods.

1. Draw your life as a river, starting at the spring or melting glacier of your birth. Where are the quiet pools, the rapids, the waterfalls?

2. Look back over your drawing of the river of your life. What patterns do you see? Do quiet pools often follow rapids? Does a vegetation-clogged segment end in a beaver dam and a small trickle?

Tracing the Theme

Like the water and the words that Norman and his father speak of, story and theme are almost inextricably intertwined. The narrator in Joseph Conrad's *Heart of Darkness* comments on this interrelationship when he describes two types of stories, one told by seamen, the other told by Marlow.

> The yarns of seamen have a direct simplicity, the whole meaning of which lies within the shell of a cracked nut. But Marlow was not typical (if his propensity to spin yarns be excepted), and to him the meaning of an episode was not inside like a kernel but outside, enveloping the tale which brought it out only as a glow brings out a haze, in the likeness of one of these misty halos that sometimes are made visible by the spectral illumination of moonshine.[2]

Commenting on the close relationship of story and theme, John Gardner wrote in *The Art of Fiction*, "Theme is not imposed on the story but evoked from within it."[3] The tale reveals the theme like "a glow brings out a haze." Theme springs from within the story itself. But in the case of life stories, we can take this one step further. Certainly you discover theme by studying your stories, but theme is more elemental than story. Themes are the words under the water of story; they are the deeper truths. Stories shape our lives as boulders and trees shape a river. But stories also flow over us and are shaped by who we truly are. Themes are generalizations, but we approach them through the particular details of a story. The story simply embodies theme and gives it a shape in the same way rapids in a river reveal the stones lying beneath the churning water.

But what is theme? It is more than the topic, more than what the story is about. *A River Runs Through It* has topics of fly-fishing and religion and brothers whom you love but can't save from themselves. Other stories have topics such as racism in the South *(To Kill a Mockingbird),* a holiday in an Italian castle *(Enchanted April),* and running a coffee plantation in Africa *(Out of Africa).* But you could hear several stories about a holiday in the same Italian castle, and all could have different themes. Likewise, stories with similar themes can have wildly varying topics.

Theme is what is made of the topic; it's the view of life expressed by the author. It is what the story has to say about the topic.[4] Two stories may have the same topic but differ significantly in their meaning and their feel. The topic may be a birthday party when you turned seven, but the theme is how your mother always used those events to showcase her skills in throwing a smashing party. So the event became more about her than about you. Or perhaps the theme had to do with how you were so shy that you didn't invite people to the party for fear they wouldn't show up. The theme is what the story has to say about the idea contained within it, the meaning with which the author grapples. Theme answers the questions: "What does this all add up to? What does it mean?" The theme is the subtext of the story, the real meaning behind the events and characters. It is the words under the water.

> The Mississippi's mighty but it starts in Minnesota at a place where you could walk across with five steps down.
> —Indigo Girls, "Ghost," *Rites of Passage* CD

Sometimes themes are expressed in single words—courage, powerlessness, friendship—but a single word does not address the issue of what the author thinks about the theme. More than simply a concept or idea explored in the story, a theme asserts some truth, and as such it is better expressed in a sentence. One theme of *A River Runs Through It* is, "You can love completely without complete understanding."[5]

3. Think about "The Three Little Pigs" and "Hansel and Gretl." List some of the stories' themes (for example: ingenuity, diligence), then write them in a sentence (for example: "He who takes the time to do something well won't be served for dinner").

If our stories are like paintings, then the paintings are impressionistic. There is value in looking closely at the brushstrokes, but to get a feel for the whole, you must stand back ten feet. To see theme, we step back from the stories and look at them from a distance. Sometimes it also helps to let the Labrador retriever of your memory run amok in the art gallery and see what he brings back. Skim chapter 6 in *To Be Told.*

4. Look back through the stories you have written so far and at your well of stories. What themes do you notice?

5. Think of your stories in terms of paintings. What colors do you see and what does each represent? Perhaps you sense red in the stories, and to you red signifies violent anger. Maybe there's yellow, and for you yellow indicates airiness and insubstantiality.

*6. What do the themes and patterns of your life reveal about God? For instance: "My story reveals a surprising and unpredictable God who transforms shame through foolishness, violence through kindness, and arrogance through weakness."[6]

Theme does not tie everything in a bow, but it does start to connect the pieces of the story and make more sense of them. Theme develops gradually as we read the novel or live our lives. Our experiences reveal meaning, and our stories are the images of that meaning. So we must play with our stories until theme reveals itself and connections occur. As Sherlock Holmes observed, "It is a capital mistake to theorize before one has data. Insensibly one begins to twist facts to suit theories, instead of theories to suit facts."[7] Don't force theme. Simply let the Labrador worry it a bit and sniff around for recurring images and patterns.

The work we have done so far can be put in the form of equations. If you take a particular person with particular characteristics and put him or her in a particular setting, something will happen. That is the scene. Each scene has a plot, and you can add up the scenes to discover the overarching plot. Within these scenes and plot you will find theme.

character + setting = scene

scene + scene + scene = plot

plot reveals theme

Everything—character, setting, scenes, and overarching plot, as well as other elements such as metaphors—works together to reveal theme.

BUILDING AN ALTAR OF STORIES

Writer Norman Maclean calls *A River Runs Through It* a love poem to his family. In this novella, he explores how a person can love someone without understanding him

or being able to save him from himself. Maclean uses story to honor his family by looking honestly at both the beauty and the tragedy of their lives.

God uses stories as his primary method of communication with us. These narratives establish our identity: We are God's sheep, his children, his bride. He is faithful
and loving in spite of the fact that we are not. When the Israelites decided to create a
golden calf and worship it (see Exodus 32), they did so because they forgot who they
were and who God is. Because of this tendency toward forgetfulness, God instructs us
to remember stories, and he frequently provides symbols to encapsulate them. He
tells his people to eat bread made without yeast for seven days, to set aside an omer
of manna, or to write something on a scroll (see Exodus
12:14-15, 16:32, 17:14). Each of these actions was designed to remind the people of a time when God had
worked powerfully on their behalf. When life became bleak,
they could look at these signs and remember the stories of
God's care for them.

Throughout the Old Testament, God seems particu-
larly concerned with passing on stories to future generations. He commanded the Israelites to commemorate the

> And she said, It's okay that you can't
> get over it. Maybe you never will.
> Maybe that hole will never fill. She
> said, Maybe your learning to leave it
> empty is the meaning of your life.
>
> —HEATHER HARPHAM,
> *I Went to the Animal Fair*

Feast of the Unleavened Bread. "And when your children ask you, 'What does this ceremony mean to you?' then tell them, 'It is the Passover sacrifice to the LORD, who
passed over the houses of the Israelites in Egypt and spared our homes when he struck
down the Egyptians'" (Exodus 12:26-27). Psalm 78 explains the purpose of this retelling: "Then they would put their trust in God and would not forget his deeds but
would keep his commands. They would not be like their forefathers—a stubborn and
rebellious generation, whose hearts were not loyal to God, whose spirits were not faithful to him" (verses 7-8). Such symbols—and the stories they represent—called the
Israelites to faith, hope, and love.

Joshua 4 tells about another symbol used to spark memory—that of picking up
stones from the dry riverbed and creating an altar—and its attendant story of the long-
awaited crossing of the Jordan into the Promised Land. For the Israelites of Joshua's day

and for successive generations, the Jordan stones helped explain why things were the way they were. Joshua stated this explicitly when he said to the people, "In the future when your descendants ask their fathers, 'What do these stones mean?' tell them, 'Israel crossed the Jordan on dry ground.'" Joshua went on to explain that it was God who dried up both the Jordan and the Red Sea (see 4:21-23). The stones symbolized the crossing of the twelve tribes, served as a reminder of God's incredible power, and explained how the Israelites came to be in Canaan.

> God does not delay to hear our prayers because He has no mind to give; but that, by enlarging our desires, He may give us the more largely.
>
> —Saint Anselm

After you gather the stones of your stories from the middle of your Jordan River, you can begin to build your altars to God's faithfulness. Study the story stones; look for common elements and themes. Then use these story stones to construct theme altars. One altar might be made up of story stones that tell of God's provision. Another might recount places where he was terribly absent. One might be an altar of betrayal; another one, joy. Your altars may be built with stories of redemption as well as stories where shalom remains shattered. At these altars we recall how God has worked in the past, just as we hope for God to work in the future.

7. What theme altars would you like to build? Which story stones will you use to build them?

After the Israelites stacked their twelve stones into a pillar, Joshua explained that the stones served a dual purpose: to be "a sign among [them]" and "a memorial to the people of Israel forever" (Joshua 4:6-7). A more complete explanation comes later in the chapter: The stones are a reminder so that "you might always fear the LORD your God." Also, the stones will prove to "all the peoples of the earth" that "the hand of the

LORD is powerful" (4:24). Indeed, when the Amorite and Canaanite kings "heard how the LORD had dried up the Jordan before the Israelites until we had crossed over, their hearts melted and they no longer had the courage to face the Israelites" (5:1).

The Jordan itself was a boundary between a people that wanders in the desert and a people that has a homeland. The crossing of the Jordan marked Israel's transformation into nationhood, and the altar reminded the people of this fulfillment of God's promise.

The ark, too, was a tangible reminder of God's character and his covenant with us. The ark of the covenant of the Lord is mentioned seven times in Joshua 4. The reference becomes a refrain that reminds us again and again that God intends to fulfill his promises. Inside the ark is another symbol, a jar of manna (see Exodus 16:33-34), which is a reminder of God's grace toward and provision for his people. So there's a symbol (the omer of manna) inside a symbol (the ark) that crosses a symbol (the Jordan), all of which are commemorated by a symbol (the altar made of stones collected from the riverbed). The symbols pile up much like the water of the Jordan itself and, when released, create a flood of stories.

This flood leads the storyteller to recall the incident forty years earlier when the Israelites refused to cross the Jordan, which would lead back to a description of wandering in the wilderness, crossing the Red Sea, witnessing the plagues, being rescued from slavery, and serving as slaves for four hundred years in Egypt. The stories of God's faithfulness domino back on each other through hundreds of years. But even that is not really the beginning. With the images of the ark of the covenant, crossings, miracles, and large bodies of water, the crossing of the Jordan is reminiscent of the story of Noah's ark, which also provided a way for God's chosen to navigate deadly waters. The story of crossing the Jordan into the Promised Land ripples back through nearly the entire history of humankind.

God repeatedly uses tangible objects as reminders. He invests objects with meaning to jostle our memories when we become forgetful. So you may find it helpful to choose stones—or a picture, a candle, or some other object—to symbolize the story altars you build. Through these objects, allow your stories to inhabit your everyday life. One symbol that hints of passion to me (Lisa) is a rock with a vein running through it. It's an ugly rock, and that ugliness reminds me of how hard and unlovely life can be. But someone took the trouble to grind through it and found crystals inside. The rock is a geode, but unless you know what geodes look like, you would never guess it could hold such beauty within it. The rock reminds me that sometimes it takes a lot of painful grinding through stone to find passion. And, like the crystals that reflect light with their sharp angles and planes, what you find often has a terrible beauty to it.

8. What objects have become symbols of your stories for you?

*9. Write one of these stories.

LETTING YOUR CALLING FIND YOU

Scoop your stories from the bottom of the river and let the water slosh around in the pan until you wash all the silt away. Then poke at the story stones with your finger and look for the telltale glitter. Show the contents of your pan to other story-miners who can help you distinguish the pyrite from the gold. Ask them what themes they see in your pan. What passions? What deep wounds? What great joys and delights? Scoop up some more stories and see if they follow the same patterns or new ones. Look for the wounds that cause you to shout, "No!" and the joys that cause you to call out, "Yes!" When you know these, you can begin to dream. And your core dreams will always involve bringing justice, reconciliation, and hope to others.

*10. What wrongs do you dream of righting? What good do you dream of growing?

11. In what ways do you nourish your dreams? How do you hamper them?

Read chapters 7 and 8, "Writing Your Destiny" and "Editing Together," in *To Be Told.* Your stories will guide you in the process of letting your calling find you. Your calling may involve being a single mom who works long hours at an unsatisfying job in order to provide for her children. Or it may include living in an upper-middle-class neighborhood and playing tennis at the club. Or it may mean working in a village in Uganda with children orphaned by AIDS. Contexts vary and so does the ease of living life, but calling is not primarily about where we live or what we do. Calling is about *how* we do it. In the how, we reveal the character we are to play and the picture of God we are to make known to others. A orphanage worker in Uganda might reveal God's reckless love through giving up most comforts to serve a broken world. The tennis-playing, upper-middle-class man might be called to reveal God's

> No one means all he says, and yet very few say all they mean, for words are slippery and thought is viscous.
>
> —HENRY ADAMS, *The Education of Henry Adams*

wild abandon through both the joy he experiences on the court and the level of honesty with which he confesses his struggles and pursues the hearts of his companions. The single mom may reveal God's patient love through her kindness toward her children, her refusal to gossip and complain at work, and her relentless pursuit of education that will enable her to get a better job.

No calling is more honorable than any other. How we respond to the call is what matters. If the single mom is bitter and cynical, if the tennis-playing man is unconcerned about others, if the orphanage worker is self-righteous, they dishonor their callings. Honoring their callings may involve speaking about issues of the heart with tennis buddies at the country club or tenderly caring for a child dying of AIDS. Our callings have specificity: we enact our dreams on behalf of a particular people, in a certain place, to solve a problem, using a specific process.

To whom, where, and what are you called and how are you to accomplish your calling? You probably don't know the answers to all these questions, but answering the ones you do know will help you glimpse the trajectory of your calling.

12. Whom do you feel called to serve? To which specific populations are you drawn?

13. Where are you to be? To what city, region, nation, and culture are you called?

14. What are your burdens? What needs (social, financial, physical, psychological, intellectual, creative, spiritual, legal, recreational) are you called to serve? You may find it helpful to look back at your answers regarding your passion in chapter 5 of this workbook.

15. What are you to do? How are you to engage? Through prayer, administration, teaching, counseling, painting, building, dancing, cooking, nursing, or something else?

Your themes, passions, and calling will lead you to your mission statement. "A good mission statement takes years to form and can't be finalized without the hard work of reading your past and imagining your future. Developing a mission statement requires unearthing your desire, articulating your passion, and following the bent of your life story as God has written it."[8] You may only have a vague inkling of your mission statement right now. Just remember, it's a work in progress.

16. List your life goals (for example: going on a long vacation, starting a Bible study in your neighborhood, teaching English to immigrants, buying a house, reading the classics, saving for retirement, learning Spanish, starting a shelter for battered women).

17. Write a mission statement or some phrases of a mission statement (for example: "training truthtellers to embrace stories that transform the way we relate to others."[9]).

18. How does your mission statement impact your life goals?

19. Look over the stories you've written and pick one with a theme that intrigues you. Then write another story from your life that deals with the same theme.

For Discussion in Your Story Group—Meeting 8

As you become more aware of themes in people's stories and see patterns in the ways they interact in the group, be careful to share this information kindly. Too often insight is used as a bludgeon to try to shame or force the other person to change.

Be aware, too, that there can be a subtle difference between naming a pattern kindly and naming it with malice. So before you speak, listen to your feelings toward that person. Ask yourself why you want to name the pattern. Is it for your sake or for the other person's sake? Your story group should be a place of honesty, but only if that honesty is infused with equal portions of tenderness and humility. If the group becomes a place of honesty with brutality, it has failed terribly.

> I'm not concerned with the facts, but everything here is the truth.
>
> —James Autry

1. In the group, answer these questions:
   - Do you embrace and have gratitude for your current situation? Why or why not?
   - Do you take responsibility for both the world you have been given and that which you have created? Why or why not?
   - How do your story and mission play out in your life?[10]
2. Think back through all the stories that each person has brought to the group. (Ask members to provide brief reminders, if necessary.) What themes do you see running through the stories? Do these overlap with the themes the person listed in response to question 4, earlier in this chapter?
3. Have each person read a story. What is a theme of the story?

Your Well of Stories

As you worked through the chapter, the questions may have reminded you of other scenes. Add these to your well of stories to write later.

chapter nine

telling our stories in community

"You must see your sisters and tell them about your mother's death," says Auntie Ying. "But most important, you must tell them about her life. The mother they did not know, they must now know."

"See my sisters, tell them about my mother," I say, nodding. "What will I say? What can I tell them about my mother? I don't know anything. She was my mother."

The aunties are looking at me as if I had become crazy right before their eyes.

"Not know your own mother?" cries Auntie An-mei with disbelief. "How can you say? Your mother is in your bones!"

"Tell them stories of your family here. How she became success," offers Auntie Lin.

"Tell them stories she told you, lessons she taught, what you know about her mind that has become your mind," says Auntie Ying. "You mother very smart lady."

I hear more choruses of "Tell them, tell them" as each auntie frantically tries to think what should be passed on.

"Her kindness."

"Her smartness."

"Her dutiful nature to family."

"Her hopes, things that matter to her."

"The excellent dishes she cooked."

"Imagine, a daughter not knowing her own mother!"

And then it occurs to me. They are frightened. In me, they see their own daughters, just as ignorant, just as unmindful of all the truths and hopes they have brought to America. They see daughters who grow impatient when their mothers talk in Chinese, who think they are stupid when they explain things in fractured English. They see that joy and luck do not mean the same to their daughters, that to these closed American-born minds "joy luck" is not a word, it does not exist. They see daughters who will bear grandchildren born without any connecting hope passed from generation to generation.

—AMY TAN, *The Joy Luck Club*

While she was still in China, Jing-Mei's mother started the Joy Luck Club as a place to feast on both food and stories during a time of desperate poverty and war. Years later, after Jing-Mei's mother dies, the aunties locate Jing-Mei's twin half-sisters in China and give Jing-Mei money so she can travel to meet them. The aunties want Jing-Mei to tell her half-sisters about the mother they never knew, to pass on her mother's stories. They invite Jing-Mei to a story feast.

TELLING STORIES IN COMMUNITY

Stories are meant to be told. Writing your stories is a gift you give yourself. Telling them is a gift you give others. By telling your stories, you offer a bit of yourself in a world of small talk, pager messages, and e-mail. You offer others a glimpse of what it means to be human and of the struggles that are common to us all, and you invite others into community. The triune God models that community for us. Father, Son, and Holy Spirit have one another, but they want more, and so God created humans, beings with whom he could share the story of his love and the joy of community. God told his story to us, and he calls us to tell our own stories.

Yes, you take a risk when you tell your stories. Others may not respond kindly or with compassion. They may feel that your stories are an unnecessary burden on them. They may even judge you and decide that your friendship is not worth it. God took the same risk in creating us. He shared his story with us and gave us the freedom to choose to be a part of it…or not. Certainly you must choose wisely those to whom you tell your stories. Some people might use your stories to harm you. Even well-chosen people may at times fail to listen well. Telling our stories will always be a risk, but the alternative is a life that lacks the richness that comes with deep, life-changing relationships.

In giving the gift of your stories, you also receive. Reading your stories in community gives you the opportunity to hear your stories through the ears of others. The people who hear your story will point out things you didn't see and ask you questions about things you haven't considered. By sharing your stories with others, you invite them to look more closely at your life, themes, calling, and passions, at what propels you forward and what hinders you. You invite them to edit with you. If you edit well, your stories will be transformed.

John Byng-Hall, a therapist and researcher in the area of family stories, says, "If I get [clients] to retell the stories at the end of the therapy, they tend to do so in a different way, which is less moralizing, less rigid, less splitting into good and bad. We end up with a more real picture of people with both strengths and weaknesses."[1] This transformation involves writing honestly about painful events instead of cushioning their impact by either diminishing the harm done or excusing our own actions or those of others. The transformation also leads us to recognize the exquisite beauty of God's handiwork in us. Transformation involves writing our stories with honesty and grace, truth and love, faith and hope—and being willing to let those remain in tension instead of canceling each other out.

> Through the power that memory gives us of thinking, feeling, imagining our way back through time we can at long last finally finish with the past in the sense of removing its power to hurt us and other people and to stunt our growth as human beings.
>
> —FREDERICK BUECHNER, *Telling Secrets*

Read chapters 9 and 10, "Story Feasting" and "Prayer That Reveals," in *To Be Told.*

1. In what contexts do you feast on stories (for example: family gatherings, small group at church)? What kinds of stories do you tell?

*2. Where do you tell your most painful stories, and with whom are you most vulnerable? Why?

Celebrating in Community

We often feast to celebrate good endings: birthdays, graduation, job promotions, holidays, the Sabbath. Like denouements, these are not final endings but simply resting points along the way. Each of these small endings and celebrations gives us a glimpse of the perfect ending we long for: the new heaven and new earth. Each offers an imperfect view of the perfect meal: the wedding feast of the Lamb. At that celebration, even our most painful stories will be redeemed. In the meantime, the hope for redemption entices us to imagine how God might transform those stories. "We will only love our story to the degree that we see the glory that seeps through our most significant shattering."[2] As we catch glimpses of God's redemption, we will come to love our stories.

> The deeper that sorrow carves into your being, the more joy you can contain. Is not the cup that holds your wine the very cup that was burned in the potter's oven?
>
> —Kahlil Gibran, *The Prophet*

For some, this idea of loving our stories will be almost too painful to consider. Love that my next-door neighbor abused me when I was seven? Love that my child has cancer? Love that my wife committed adultery? Love that I struggle with anxiety and depression? We are not to love the evil that wrote the brokenness in our lives, but we can come to love how God uses these stories to soften our hearts and make us more dependent on him. Love will win. There will not be even a scrap of our story that God does not use for the cause of love and his good work in our lives.

Look back over the "What Sort of Ending Are You Writing" section in chapter 1 of *To Be Told* as well as the "Denouement" section in chapter 3 of *To Be Told*.

3. "Endings are meant to be a sensual, wild fullness of all that came before."[3] In your own life, how do you celebrate a satisfying close to one of your stories?

4. What big and small endings—denouements—have you celebrated well? Give an example or two.

5. "Perhaps one of the reasons you and I don't party well is that we don't know what to do with the tragedies that linger in our life.… When do we celebrate a denouement related to the struggle of being overweight, unwanted, angry, lonely, fearful, or ashamed? We don't. Can you imagine receiving an invitation to a party: 'Join me in celebration of no longer believing I am stupid'?"[4] If you were to invite friends to a redemption party for one of your tragedies, what would your invitation say?

6. In which of your painful stories have you seen redemption?

*7. Write one of your stories of redemption.

*8. Which stories do you most desire for God to redeem? Over what stories do you continue to wrestle with the Lord?

WRESTLING WITH GOD

At its best, prayer is a cry for personal and corporate transformation, for hearts that are both tenderer and stronger. Prayer is a plea for God to take the stories that were meant for evil and use them for good, to write something beautiful out of tragedy. This kind of prayer clings to hope in order to step farther into, instead of away from, the pain. Facing the pain may not be what you expect. For a battered woman, stepping into the pain probably means leaving the man who is harming her and facing the financial, emotional, and social poverty that will follow. God uses the pain to make us stronger and more compassionate for the sake of those who suffer. "Remove anguish and you

> Batter my heart, three-personed God; for you / As yet but knock, breathe, shine, and seek to mend.
>
> —JOHN DONNE, "Holy Sonnet #14"

remove mercy. Erase anger and you erase a hunger for justice. Jesus doesn't take away anguish and anger; he transforms heartache to passion and anger to righteous defiance."[5] But for that transformation to take place, we must first wrestle with God.

9. What is your deepest prayer?

10. What parts of your story are laced with such shame that you will not wrestle with God over them?

11. Write one of these, but only if you can remain kind and gentle toward yourself as you do.

12. When have you seen God use your heartache for the good of another person?

When we enter the agony of our souls, we learn more about ourselves and about a good God who for some reason allows evil to exist but who also works to redeem it. In dire circumstances, as we suffer emotionally or physically, we find out who we are and whom we worship. The word *cholah* in Hebrew means "to writhe in pain," and it is used to refer to childbirth and other times of extreme agony.

> I hear a cry as of a woman in labor,
>> a groan *[cholah]* as of one bearing her first child—
> the cry of the Daughter of Zion gasping for breath,
>> stretching out her hands and saying,
> "Alas! I am fainting;
>> my life is given over to murderers."
>>> (Jeremiah 4:31)

Micah also says that the daughter of Zion *cholah*s (see 4:10); God's people *cholah* (see Isaiah 26:17); and God *cholah*s on our behalf (see Deuteronomy 32:18). The bizarre, painful paradox is that *cholah* also means "dance," usually a dance of celebration: "When the men were returning home after David had killed the Philistine, the women came out from all the towns of Israel to meet King Saul with singing and dancing *[cholah]*, with joyful songs and with tambourines and lutes" (1 Samuel 18:6). To celebrate the end of the Lord's judgment, his people *cholah* in Jeremiah 31:4.

> I will build you up again
>> and you will be rebuilt, O Virgin Israel.
> Again you will take up your tambourines
>> and go out to dance *[cholah]* with the joyful.

What is the difference between writhing in pain and dancing? How far is it from laughing to crying? They look and feel very similar. Both lead to exhaustion, yet dancing and laughing lead to an exhaustion that is restful, while writhing leads to an exhaustion that decimates. God writhes and dances on our behalf, and he turns our writhing into dancing. When we write well the story of our pain and wrestle with the God who allowed it to happen, our dancing becomes more passionate and free. Deepening the well of sorrow deepens the well of joy. We have less to lose because we have already tasted deep loss and survived. We have tasted redemption and can dance while we wait for the rest of our tragedies to be redeemed.

How Do You Write?

We write our stories to learn what they have to teach us, but a story is sometimes an exploration of a hostile land. In those cases writing will be arduous. And sometimes the writing is writhing.

I (Lisa) recently called Selby, an editor and writer friend, and informed him about my writing woes. I have edited and written for a dozen years, I told him. I have two degrees in literature. Yet putting even a word on the page can be a herculean feat. It feels like bleeding on paper. When does it get easier? Why is it always so painful? He told me in a way that made me laugh that I was letting the whiny voice out. All writers labor over writing. In fact, a writer has been defined as someone who struggles with writing. Usually it takes financial terror to propel writers' fingers to the keyboard.

Your words may dance or writhe across the page. The process may become easier for you as you keep writing, or it may turn torturous as you delve into certain stories. Either way, it's important for you to approach writing with compassion toward the person you were in those stories. God gives us grace, so who are we to deny ourselves this grace? As you write, ask yourself if you are curious about and open to your stories. Do you feel kind toward yourself in the stories, or is there contempt for your failures or inability to protect yourself from harm? When you detect contempt, stop and regroup. Then rewrite. Ask your story community where they hear contempt in your stories.

Pay attention, too, to how you tell your stories. Are you telling your audience what

> I do not care for stories that are so tight. Stories should be like life, slightly frayed at the edges, full of loose ends and lives juxtaposed by accident rather than some grand design. Most of life has no meaning. So it must surely be a distortion of life to tell tales in which every single element is meaningful. How terrible to see a meaning or a great import in everything around one, everything one does, everything that happens to one.
>
> —SALMAN RUSHDIE, quoted in *The Novels of Salman Rushdie*

to think and feel or allowing them to experience the story for themselves? Are you giving enough detail so that the reader/listener has a feel for the setting and characters?

13. What stands in the way of your writing? What propels your fingers to the keyboard or paper?

One danger of writing our stories and looking for meaning is the trap of overspiritualizing, of finding significance in every detail. This is merely another way to diminish heartache and, ultimately, God by forcing a pattern and meaning onto all events of our lives. It does not leave room for God to be God in all his mystery and transcendence. It arrogantly assumes that the creature can fathom the Creator. We can never fully understand the meaning of any of our stories. In writing our stories, we search for patterns, but not for the pattern that takes away all mystery and makes God into a magic genie who does our bidding. We must resist cheap hope in order to hope for something unimaginably good from the hand of the One who is beyond our understanding.

> You give but little when you give of your possessions. It is when you give of yourself that you truly give.
> —Kahlil Gibran, *The Prophet*

14. Are you more likely to overspiritualize and embrace shallow hope or to despair of any meaning in your stories? Why?

15. By now, you have written more than a half-dozen of your stories. Look back over your well of stories. Which ones are you avoiding?

16. Choose one of those and write it.

FOR DISCUSSION IN YOUR STORY GROUP—MEETING 9

As you listen to the stories of others in your group, keep in mind some questions to ask yourself:

1. What is absent that needs to be present? That is, what has been left unsaid? Are there missing characters? Are there gaps in time? Is the narrator emotionally and physically present in the story?

2. What is present that needs to be absent? What is hiding behind excessive verbiage? Can words or sentences be cut in order to make the story clearer? What needs to be explored in more detail and what can be summarized so you don't bog down in details?

3. How does this story interact with and shed light on the reader's other stories? What are the overarching themes?

4. What do the stories suggest to you about the reader's calling? What passions and heartaches does the story reveal?

5. What does the story's subtext tell you? At what points does the reader's voice catch with emotion? When do you hear contempt in his or her voice? What parts of the story does the person wish to pass over quickly? Where do the events of the story and the reader's emotion or lack of it seem mismatched? Did the reader write and read the story in a way that shows kindness toward herself or himself?

As a group, discuss the following:

1. Answer question 3 from this chapter. "Endings are meant to be a sensual, wild fullness of all that came before."[6] How do you celebrate a satisfying close to one of your stories?

2. Which of your stories has been the most difficult for you to read to the group? Why?

3. Answer question 12 from this chapter: When have you seen God use your heartache for the good of another person?

4. Have each person read a story of denouement. Where in each story do you see rest? awe? gratitude? What is a theme of each story?

If your next meeting is the last time your story group will gather, you might want to add a feast of food to your final feast of stories. Build more time into the next meeting so you can eat and say good-bye.

Your Well of Stories

As you worked through the chapter, the questions may have reminded you of other scenes. Add these to your well of stories to write later.

fasting, giving, and playing with our stories

Having placed in my mouth sufficient bread for three minutes' chewing, I withdrew my powers of sensual perception and retired into the privacy of my mind, my eyes and face assuming a vacant and preoccupied expression. I reflected on the subject of my spare-time literary activities. One beginning and one ending for a book was a thing I did not agree with. A good book may have three openings entirely dissimilar and inter-related only in the prescience of the author, or for that matter one hundred times as many endings.

Examples of three separate openings—the first: The Pooka MacPhellimey, a member of the devil class, sat in his hut in the middle of a firwood meditating on the nature of the numerals and segregating in his mind the odd ones from the even. He was seated at his diptych or ancient two-leaved hinged writing-table with inner sides waxed. His rough long-nailed fingers toyed with a snuff-box of perfect rotundity and through a gap in his teeth he whistled a civil cavatina. He was a courtly man and received honour by reason of the generous treatment he gave his wife, one of the Corrigans of Carlow.

The second opening: There was nothing unusual in the appearance of Mr. John Furriskey but actually he had one distinction that is rarely encountered—he was born at the age of twenty-five and entered the world with a memory but without personal experience to account for it. His teeth were well-formed but stained by tobacco, with two molars filled and a cavity threatened in the left canine. His knowledge of physics was moderate and extended to Boyle's Law and the Parallelogram of Forces.

The third opening: Finn Mac Cool was a legendary hero of old Ireland…

—FLANN O'BRIEN, *At Swim-Two-Birds*

Who says a story can't have three beginnings? Who says it must be linear? In Flann O'Brien's zany novel *At Swim-Two-Birds,* he plays with narrative form and thumbs his nose at the conventions of storytelling. The narrator, a suspiciously idle university student and aspiring novelist, balks at the normal constraints imposed on books. He writes a novel about Dermot Trellis, who also lounges around in bed and who is himself writing a book about the corrupting powers of vice. Trellis creates his characters full-grown and requires that they live with him at the Red Swan Hotel. Because they dislike being forced to participate in Trellis's didactic stories, they drug him. While Trellis sleeps, John Furriskey gets married, buys a house, and opens a sweets shop. Then he and the other characters dash back to their assigned places before the author awakens and discovers what's afoot. So O'Brien writes about a student who writes about Trellis who writes about Furriskey and company who do some writing of their own.

PLAYING WITH OUR STORIES

We, too, have an Author who often writes stories we would not have chosen. But this Author does not loll about in bed all day. He writes with an agenda, but that agenda is for our good. He promises that, no matter what seems to be true right now, the story has a glorious ending. And he secured that glorious ending by entering the story himself in the person of Jesus. God writes the story and lives it.

Then God honors us by handing us the pen. He eagerly watches to see what we will create. He allows us to write him out of the story if we so choose. But he remains on the porch, nose pressed against the screen door, mischief in his eyes, waiting to be let back inside. We can choose to sneak around and write a different story as if he can't see us. Or we can engage with him, using what has been written so far to give us clues about what to write next. We can write a story that stays within the bounds of our expectations, or we can allow faith, hope, and love to explode the conventions and lure us to write outside the lines—and that is a great paradox. When we choose to write with God, he will call us to write both that which is in keeping with the themes of our lives and that which we would never have imagined or dreamed. The stories that we produce with God will require more of us and will be far more glorious than the ones we would have written alone.

> Man's maturity: to have regained the seriousness that he had as a child at play.
>
> —FRIEDRICH NIETZSCHE,
> *Beyond Good and Evil*

God, the Creator of the universe, allows us equal billing as coauthors on the title pages of our lives. He invites us to play with our stories and to look for redemption and calling in the midst of tragedy. Like *At Swim-Two-Birds,* our stories sometimes don't make sense. They are disjointed and confusing. But as we keep writing, praying, searching, and telling our stories, we will glimpse snippets of pattern and shreds of meaning.

Sometimes God's invitation to play with our stories can be distressing. Several years ago, I (Lisa) faced a significant life decision. Should I stay in a great job in a city where I had wonderful friends and a good church, or should I move three thousand miles away to pursue a graduate degree? I prayed about and discussed the decision with close friends. Should I give up everything for something that was uncertain and costly, or stay with what I knew and loved?

"I want skywriting," I told a friend. "I don't care what God wants me to do; I just want him to tell me. But he refuses to answer."

"He doesn't answer because he respects you," my friend replied.

It has been said that as we mature, God stops answering our prayers. Over the next six months God waited for me to decide what story to write. I chose the move, landed hard, and stood wide-eyed and tense in that new place. What followed was the most acutely painful year of my life. At the time I wrote in my journal, *I float in the empty blackness outside the spaceship. Those inside are unaware or unconcerned that I am gone. I rage at God for the unspeakable agony of being utterly alone. He answers by disconnecting my safety line.* It was a long time before I saw a glimmer of hope that God would use this experience for good. Now I'm glad I chose to make the leap, but at the time I felt as though I had taken up the pen but lost the book.

> We all got secrets. I got them same as everybody else—things we feel bad about and wish hadn't ever happened. Hurtful things. Long ago things. We're all scared and lonesome, but most of the time we keep it hid. It's like every one of us has lost his way so bad we don't even know which way is home any more only we're ashamed to ask. You know what would happen if we would own up we're lost and ask? Why, what would happen is we'd find out home is each other. We'd find out home is Jesus that loves us lost or found or any whichway.
>
> —Leo Bebb, in Frederick Buechner, *The Book of Bebb*

God doesn't answer all our questions, and some of our stories may remain unredeemed until we enter heaven. In C. S. Lewis's book *Till We Have Faces,* Orual, Queen of Glome, reads her complaint against the gods. She has been unfairly, even cruelly, treated, she says. She tells the story of her life, and after a while she realizes that she has been reading it over and over again. The silence that meets her accusations enrages and then silences her. Then she realizes that the response was there all along. "'I know now, Lord, why you utter no answer. You are yourself the answer. Before your face questions die away. What other answer would suffice?'" she says.[1] God does not offer us answers; he invites us to relationship.

1. Do you tend to grab the pen from God's hand so you can write, or do you refuse to take the pen at all? Explain your choice.

2. At what points in your life has God remained silent and waited for you to do the writing?

*3. Write one of those stories.

4. You have already identified some themes in your stories. What snippets of patterns and shreds of meaning do you see in the stories that don't make sense?

*5. Look back over the stories and fragments of stories that you have written. What does your life reveal about the person and character of God?

STORIES THAT CAUSE RIPPLES

We write our stories with the hope that in time they will make more sense and reveal something of God. We stack them into altars to remind ourselves of how God has worked in our lives. Piled into altars on the western bank of the Jordan River, the stones mentioned in Joshua 4 create a ripple in the river of history. They hearken back to God's promises to his people, to their history in Egypt, and even further back to Noah. And the story ripples forward as well. Jesus was baptized in the Jordan, "crossing over" into his new ministry where he proclaimed the ultimate Promised Land, the Kingdom of God.

The New Testament continues the theme of the importance of remembering. Jesus admonished his disciples to "Remember Lot's wife!" and "Remember the words I spoke to you" (Luke 17:32, John 15:20). Jesus used parables to remind us of God's truths, and the Gospels record his signs and wonders performed for the same twofold purpose: that those who hear might believe and that this belief might lead to commitment to Christ (see John 20:30-31).

Throughout the Old and New Testaments are "stones," the tangible reminders of a story that ripples on forever. God has not forgotten our need for concrete symbols. Preeminent are the empty cross and the Lord's Supper, reminders of God's sacrifice and his ultimate provision in delivering us from the Enemy. In addition, baptism is a symbol of crossing into a new life similar to the Israelites' crossing into God's place of promise. Each symbol holds the story of God's love and care for us, and each is a Jordan stone. And then, of course, there are our personal stones.

Remembering our stories is tantamount to remembering our lives and discovering their meanings. Recalling how God has been faithful in the past gives us hope for the future. God repeatedly stresses to his amnesiac people the importance of remembering. He instructs us to collect our stories from the middle of difficult situations and construct something tangible out of them to help us remember. Joshua could simply have said, "Always remember that the Lord is faithful," but a story speaks to the heart, and a symbol captures the imagination. Together they offer an indelible reminder of God and his work in our behalf.

FASTING AND GIVING

Read chapters 11 and 12, "The Fruit of Fasting" and "Giving Away Your Story," and the postscript in *To Be Told*.

Writing your stories with honesty and gentleness is a kind of fast. It requires a sacrifice of time. To engage well, you must give up other diversions that could fill your time—watching television, shopping, playing golf, mowing the yard, returning phone calls, reading the paper, crossing tasks off your list—in order to enter the terrain of loss and futility. "Fasting is not a tool to pry wisdom out of God's hands or to force needed insight about a decision. Fasting is not a tool for gaining discipline or developing piety (whatever that might be). Instead, fasting is the bulimic act of ridding ourselves of our fullness in order to attune our senses to the mysteries that swirl in and around us."[2] We can easily fill our lives with activity as we answer the clamor of things that should be done, or we can choose to ignore the din at times for the sake of listening for God's whisper.

As you've journeyed through this workbook, you have looked at your life, but have you *sat* with it? If not, set aside some time, find a safe place, and read back over the stories and bits of stories that you've written. Allow the contents of your well of stories to wash over you. Pay attention to where, in an attempt to minimize damage done, you left gaps and skipped over painful details. Look for points where you disappeared from your own story. Listen to and feel *how* you told the story, noting especially wherever you detect shame, contempt, or disgust toward yourself and others. In a story about being betrayed by a friend, for instance, do you allow yourself to feel and describe the powerlessness of anger, grief, and hurt? Or do you retreat to the buttressed safety of sneering contempt? Do you berate yourself for trusting someone who was untrustworthy? Or do you take the side of grace, which says that our desire to be loved and cherished by others is *good* even though it can lead us to a relationship where we are violated?

> We who lived in concentration camps can remember the men who walked through the huts comforting others, giving away their last piece of bread. They may have been few in number, but they offer sufficient proof that everything can be taken from a man but one thing: the last of the human freedoms—to choose one's attitude in any given set of circumstances, to choose one's own way.
>
> —VIKTOR FRANKL,
> *Man's Search for Meaning*

Can you face profound failures to love without contempt for or minimizing what you or others did? To refuse to follow the wide path of contempt is like walking along the edge of a razor. We must be constantly aware of our balance, or we will fall off into contempt toward ourselves or others. Staying on that razor's edge requires that we enter the realm of grief, and grief that is not buttressed by contempt feels wildly, achingly powerless and broken. Contempt gives us a feeling, though false, of power and control. Grief alone throws us at the feet of God, crying out for mercy.

> Benedictio: May your trails be crooked, winding, lonesome, dangerous, leading to the most amazing view. May your mountains rise into and above the clouds.
>
> —EDWARD ABBEY, *Desert Solitaire*

We must relinquish our stories to God. What others meant for evil, God meant for our good. Our contempt and disgust are simply ways to cling to parts of our stories that seem too painful or humiliating or exposing. Our contempt communicates, in essence, our belief that God is not powerful or kind enough to redeem and that we or others must continue to pay for the harm done. As long as we cling to contempt, we will not enter the humble joy of seeing God rewrite our stories for glory. God runs the ultimate monopoly: he uses *everything* to draw us to himself unless we thwart him with our contempt. Evil cannot win, and tragedy is not the final chapter since suffering, as well as joy, lead us to God.

6. What are your addictions? What fills you by deadening you to pain or joy?

7. Describe what you feel when you fast and what comes from the fast.

8. At what specific places in your stories do you hear contempt or disgust—either toward yourself or toward others?

9. Think about this statement: "We are as indebted to those who hated us and did us harm as we are to those who have gifted us with a faint reminder of God…. Those who sexually abused me…aroused in me fury and defiance against injustice. For that I am eternally grateful. I don't bless their harm, but I do thank God for how he has chosen to use that harm to mold me to live my story."[3] Who are the wrongdoers to whom you owe such a debt? What did their harm stir in your soul?

*10. Choose one of the stories you've already written and rewrite it with more honesty and greater kindness toward yourself.

Dermot Trellis, lolling abed at the Red Swan Hotel and dabbling with words, writes his stories as a didactic treatise. God, on the other hand, does not give answers but writes our stories as a means for relationship with him. Jesus came and gave the story of his life to us and for us. He invites us to respond to his gift by offering our stories to others. "To tell stories to impress or intimidate is to entrap—the opposite of telling stories to set others free. A gift-giving, liberating story tells of innocence lost, tragedy encountered, imagination employed, and the brief and glorious moments of an ending that reminds us again that our story is not finally written by us, but we coauthor it with God."[4]

11. "'Give not because you must but because you can.' Give not counting the money going out, but give with abandon and laughter."[5] When have you given your time, money, or possessions with abandon and laughter? What enabled you to do so in those instances?

12. When have your stories been acts of taking from another person rather than giving to him or her?

13. When have you given your stories as gifts?

You have embarked on a journey of stories, of your stories and God's stories and how they intersect. And of seeing God at work in the unlikeliest places. May the path continue to grant you tiny glimpses and spectacular vistas of God's passionate love, tender strength, and playful redemption. May you create an exquisitely beautiful quilt from the scraps of calico you've been given. And may you write your story—and his story in your story—with honesty and kindness.

FOR DISCUSSION IN YOUR STORY GROUP—MEETING 10

If this is the last time you will meet as a story group, plan ahead so you can end well. Be aware of how you might try to diminish the pain, and possibly relief, of ending by being disengaged, starting an argument, busying yourself with preparations, or acting as if this is just a regular meeting. Honor the group by having the courage to walk along the razor's edge of grief. Celebrate community by eating a meal together, perhaps one where everyone brings a dish with a story behind it. Then feast on food and stories. Take time to enjoy one another and to honor these people who have walked through your stories with you.

1. Have each person read a story that she or he rewrote with more honesty and greater kindness (see question 10 earlier in this chapter).

2. What stories told by other group members have impacted you the most? What have you appreciated about their feedback regarding your stories? What characteristics of God have you seen revealed in their stories?

3. What have you learned about yourself in the process of writing your stories and telling them in community?

4. Think through the themes of each person's life. What do you hope for them?

Your Well of Stories

As you worked through the chapter, the questions may have reminded you of other scenes. Add these to your well of stories to write later.

Notes

Introduction

1. Here is the complete quote: "If...I tell you that to let no day pass without discussing goodness and all the other subjects about which you hear me talking and examining both myself and others is really the very best thing that a man can do, and that life without this sort of examination is not worth living, you will be even less inclined to believe me." Socrates, "The Apology of Socrates," section 38a, in Plato, *The Last Days of Socrates,* trans. Hugh Tredennick (New York: Penguin, 1969), 71-72.

2. David Wilcox, "Show the Way," *Big Horizon* CD (Hollywood, CA: A&M Records, 1994).

Chapter 1

The epigraph to this chapter is drawn from Eliza Calvert Hall, *Aunt Jane of Kentucky* (New York: Little, Brown, 1907), 73-75.

1. Mary Oliver, "The Summer Day," *New and Selected Poems* (Boston, MA: Beacon, 1992), 94.

2. Hall, *Aunt Jane,* 75.

Chapter 2

The epigraph to this chapter is drawn from C. S. Lewis, *Till We Have Faces* (Glasgow: William Collins, 1956), 263.

1. Sam Keen, quoted in Eileen Silva Kindig, *Remember the Time...? The Power and Promise of Family Storytelling* (Downers Grove, IL: InterVarsity, 1997), 27.

2. William Faulkner, quoted in M. Thomas Inge, *Conversations with William Faulkner* (Jackson, MS: University Press of Mississippi, 1999), 180.

Chapter 3

The epigraph to this chapter is drawn from William Faulkner, *Flags in the Dust* (New York: Random House, 1973), 3.

1. Faulkner, *Flags,* 5.

2. For more on this idea, see Peggy J. Miller and Barbara Byhouwer Moore, "Narrative Conjunctions of Caregiver and Child: A Comparative Perspective on Socialization Through Stories," *Ethos* 17 (1989): 428-49. See also Elaine Reese, Catherine A. Haden, and Robyn Fivush, "Mothers, Fathers, Daughters, Sons: Gender Differences in Autobiographical Reminiscing," *Research on Language and Social Interaction* 29, no. 1 (1996): 27-56.

3. Eileen Silva Kindig, *Remember the Time…? The Power and Promise of Family Storytelling* (Downers Grove, IL: InterVarsity, 1997), 31.

4. Elizabeth Stone, *Black Sheep and Kissing Cousins: How Our Family Stories Shape Us* (New York: Times Books, 1988), 8.

5. For more on this idea, see Peggy J. Miller and others, "Personal Storytelling as a Medium of Socialization in Chinese and American Families," *Child Development* 68, no. 3 (1997): 557-68. See also Miller and Moore, "Narrative Conjunctions"; Kimberly P. Williams, "Storytelling as a Bridge to Literacy: An Examination of Personal Storytelling Among Black Middle-Class Mothers and Children," *Journal of Negro Education* 60, no. 3 (1991): 399-409; Mustafa Kemal Mirzeler, "The Formation of Male Identity and the Roots of Violence Against Women: The Case of Kurdish Songs, Stories and Storytellers," *Journal of Muslim Minority Affairs* 20, no. 2 (2000): 261-69; Chris Chance and Barbara H. Fiese, "Gender-Stereotyped Lessons About Emotion in Family Narratives," *Narrative Inquiry* 9, no. 2 (1999): 243-55; John Byng-Hall, "Scripts and Legends in Families and Family Therapy," *Family Process* 27 (1988): 167-79.

6. Daniel Taylor, *Tell Me a Story: The Life-Shaping Power of Our Stories* (New York: Doubleday, 1996), 85.

7. Faulkner, *Flags*, 14.

8. Salman Rushdie, quoted in Esther B. Fein, "Rushdie, Defying Death Threats, Suddenly Appears in New York," *New York Times,* December 12, 1991.

9. For more on this idea, see Stone, *Black Sheep*, 182.

10. For more on this idea, see Jean Peneff, "Myths in Life Stories," in *The Myths We Live By,* ed. Raphael Samuel and Paul Thompson (Florence, KY: Routledge, 1990), 36-48.

11. Mirzeler, "The Formation of Male Identity," 266.

12. John Byng-Hall, interview by Paul Thompson, "The Power of Family Myths," in *The Myths We Live By,* ed. Samuel and Thompson, 223.

13. Anthony Lane, "Back to Basics: Joe Eszterhas's 'Hollywood Animal,'" *The New Yorker,* February 9, 2004, 80.

14. See Janine Roberts, *Tales and Transformations: Stories in Families and Family Therapy* (New York: Norton, 1994), 19.

15. See Roger C. Schank, *Tell Me a Story: A New Look at Real and Artificial Memory* (New York: Scribner, 1990), 168.

16. See Stone, *Black Sheep*, 102.

Chapter 4

The epigraph to this chapter is drawn from Tim O'Brien, *The Things They Carried* (New York: Broadway, 1990), 203-4.

1. For a more in-depth discussion of issues of truth and memory, see Dan B. Allender, *The Wounded Heart* (Colorado Springs, CO: NavPress, 1995), 21-39.

2. Janet Burroway, *Writing Fiction: A Guide to Narrative Craft,* 5th ed. (New York: Longman, 2000), 305.

Chapter 5

The epigraph to this chapter is drawn from Chaim Potok, *My Name Is Asher Lev* (New York: Fawcett Crest, 1972), 11-12.

1. Saul Bellow, *Seize the Day* (New York: Penguin, 1984), 78.

2. Ray Bradbury, *The Martian Chronicles* (New York: Bantam, 1972), 14.

3. John Berendt, *Midnight in the Garden of Good and Evil* (New York: Random House, 1994), 3.

4. Alan Paton, *Cry, the Beloved Country* (New York: Macmillan, 1987), 3.

5. Harper Lee, *To Kill a Mockingbird* (New York: Warner, 1960), 9-10.

6. Dan B. Allender, *To Be Told* (Colorado Springs: WaterBrook, 2005), 62.

7. Allender, *To Be Told,* 63.

8. William Butler Yeats, "Easter 1916," *The New Oxford Book of English Verse, 1250–1950* (New York: Oxford University Press, 1972), 818-20.

Chapter 6

The epigraph to this chapter is drawn from Arundhati Roy, *The God of Small Things* (New York: HarperPerennial, 1997), 12.

1. Sir Arthur Conan Doyle, *The Complete Sherlock Holmes,* vol. 1 (Garden City, NY: Doubleday, 1930), 162.

2. For a more in-depth look at powerlessness, betrayal, and ambivalence, see Dan B. Allender, *The Wounded Heart* (Colorado Springs: NavPress, 1995), 113-56.

3. Dan B. Allender, *To Be Told* (Colorado Springs: WaterBrook, 2005), 74.

4. Valiska Gregory, *Through the Mickle Woods* (New York: Little, Brown, 1992), approximately 21.

Chapter 7

The epigraph to this chapter is drawn from Charlotte Brontë, *Jane Eyre* (New York: Bantam, 1981), 401.

1. E. M. Forster, *Aspects of the Novel* (New York: Harcourt Brace Jovanovich, 1955), 86.

2. For more on this idea, see Janet Burroway, *Writing Fiction: A Guide to Narrative Craft,* 5th ed. (New York: Longman, 2000), 33.

3. Dan B. Allender, *To Be Told* (Colorado Springs: WaterBrook, 2005), 47.

4. Allender, *To Be Told,* 48.

5. James Strong, *Strong's Exhaustive Concordance of the Bible* (McLean, VA: MacDonald).

6. Frederick Buechner, *The Magnificent Defeat* (San Francisco: HarperSanFrancisco, 1985), 18.

7. Patricia Raybon, *My First White Friend: Confessions on Race, Love, and Forgiveness* (New York: Viking, 1996), 234.

Chapter 8

The epigraph to this chapter is drawn from Norman Maclean, *A River Runs Through It* (New York: Simon & Schuster, 1976), 103-4.

1. Maclean, *River Runs Through It,* 69.

2. Joseph Conrad, *Heart of Darkness and Other Tales* (New York: Oxford University Press, 1998), 138.

3. John Gardner, *The Art of Fiction: Notes on Craft for Young Writers* (New York: Vintage, 1991), 177.

4. For more on this idea, see Janet Burroway, *Writing Fiction: A Guide to Narrative Craft,* 5th ed. (New York: Longman, 2000), 303.

5. Maclean, *River Runs Through It,* 112.

6. Dan B. Allender, *To Be Told* (Colorado Springs: WaterBrook, 2005), 121.

7. Sir Arthur Conan Doyle, *The Complete Sherlock Holmes,* vol. 1 (Garden City, NY: Doubleday, 1930), 163.

8. Allender, *To Be Told,* 119.

9. Allender, *To Be Told,* 121.

10. Allender, *To Be Told,* chapter 7.

Chapter 9

The epigraph to this chapter is drawn from Amy Tan, *The Joy Luck Club* (New York: Ivy, 1989), 30-31.

1. John Byng-Hall, interview by Paul Thompson, "The Power of Family Myths," in *The Myths We Live By,* ed. Raphael Samuel and Paul Thompson (Florence, KY: Routledge, 1990), 224.

2. Dan B. Allender, *To Be Told* (Colorado Springs: WaterBrook, 2005), 51.

3. Allender, *To Be Told,* 20.

4. Allender, *To Be Told,* 50-51.

5. Allender, *To Be Told,* 171.

6. Allender, *To Be Told,* 20.

Chapter 10

The epigraph to this chapter is drawn from Flann O'Brien, *At Swim-Two-Birds* (New York: Penguin, 1966), 9-10.

1. C. S. Lewis, *Till We Have Faces* (Glasgow: William Collins, 1956), 319.

2. Dan B. Allender, *To Be Told* (Colorado Springs: WaterBrook, 2005), 186.

3. Allender, *To Be Told,* 205.

4. Allender, *To Be Told,* 206.

5. Allender, *To Be Told,* 203.

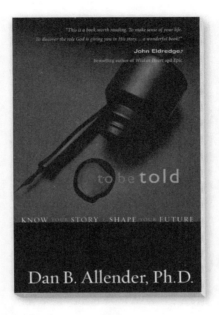

As we read our past and gain clarity from the themes that God has written into our life, we can discover how God is leading us into a more fulfilling future.

Also Available from Dan B. Allender, Ph.D.

Available in bookstores and from online retailers

WATERBROOK PRESS

www.waterbrookpress.com